MACMILLAN MASTER GUIDES

GENERAL EDITOR: JAMES GIBSON

Published

JANE AUSTEN	*Emma* Norman Page
	Sense and Sensibility Judy Simons
	Pride and Prejudice Raymond Wilson
	Mansfield Park Richard Wirdnam
SAMUEL BECKETT	*Waiting for Godot* Jennifer Birkett
WILLIAM BLAKE	*Songs of Innocence* and *Songs of Experience* Alan Tomlinson
ROBERT BOLT	*A Man for all Seasons* Leonard Smith
EMILY BRONTË	*Wuthering Heights* Hilda D. Spear
GEOFFREY CHAUCER	*The Miller's Tale* Michael Alexander
	The Pardoner's Tale Geoffrey Lester
	The Prologue to the Canterbury Tales Nigel Thomas and Richard Swan
CHARLES DICKENS	*Bleak House* Dennis Butts
	Great Expectations Dennis Butts
	Hard Times Norman Page
GEORGE ELIOT	*Middlemarch* Graham Handley
	Silas Marner Graham Handley
	The Mill on the Floss Helen Wheeler
HENRY FIELDING	*Joseph Andrews* Trevor Johnson
E. M. FORSTER	*Howards End* Ian Milligan
	A Passage to India Hilda D. Spear
WILLIAM GOLDING	*The Spire* Rosemary Sumner
	Lord of the Flies Raymond Wilson
OLIVER GOLDSMITH	*She Stoops to Conquer* Paul Ranger
THOMAS HARDY	*The Mayor of Casterbridge* Ray Evans
	Tess of the D'Urbervilles James Gibson
	Far from the Madding Crowd Colin Temblett-Wood
JOHN KEATS	*Selected Poems* John Garrett
PHILIP LARKIN	*The Whitsun Weddings* and *The Less Deceived* Andrew Swarbrick
D. H. LAWRENCE	*Sons and Lovers* R. P. Draper
HARPER LEE	*To Kill a Mockingbird* Jean Armstrong
CHRISTOPHER MARLOWE	*Doctor Faustus* David A. Male
THE METAPHYSICAL POETS	Joan van Emden

MACMILLAN MASTER GUIDES

THOMAS MIDDLETON and WILLIAM ROWLEY	*The Changeling* Tony Bromham
ARTHUR MILLER	*The Crucible* Leonard Smith
GEORGE ORWELL	*Animal Farm* Jean Armstrong
WILLIAM SHAKESPEARE	*Richard II* Charles Barber *Hamlet* Jean Brooks *King Lear* Francis Casey *Henry V* Peter Davison *The Winter's Tale* Diana Devlin *Julius Caesar* David Elloway *Macbeth* David Elloway *Measure for Measure* Mark Lilly *Henry IV Part I* Helen Morris *Romeo and Juliet* Helen Morris *The Tempest* Kenneth Pickering *A Midsummer Night's Dream* Kenneth Pickering
GEORGE BERNARD SHAW	*St Joan* Leonée Ormond
RICHARD SHERIDAN	*The School for Scandal* Paul Ranger *The Rivals* Jeremy Rowe
ALFRED TENNYSON	*In Memoriam* Richard Gill
JOHN WEBSTER	*The White Devil* and *The Duchess of Malfi* David A. Male

Forthcoming

CHARLOTTE BRONTË	*Jane Eyre* Robert Miles
JOHN BUNYAN	*The Pilgrim's Progress* Beatrice Batson
JOSEPH CONRAD	*The Secret Agent* Andrew Mayne
T. S. ELIOT	*Murder in the Cathedral* Paul Lapworth *Selected Poems* Andrew Swarbrick
GERARD MANLEY HOPKINS	*Selected Poems* R. Watt
BEN JONSON	*Volpone* Michael Stout
RUDYARD KIPLING	*Kim* Leonée Ormond
ARTHUR MILLER	*Death of a Salesman* Peter Spalding
JOHN MILTON	*Comus* Tom Healy
WILLIAM SHAKESPEARE	*Othello* Tony Bromham *As You Like It* Kiernan Ryan *Coriolanus* Gordon Williams *Antony and Cleopatra* Martin Wine
ANTHONY TROLLOPE	*Barchester Towers* Ken Newton
VIRGINIA WOOLF	*To the Lighthouse* John Mepham *Mrs Dalloway* Julian Pattison
W. B. YEATS	*Selected Poems* Stan Smith

MACMILLAN MASTER GUIDES

WAITING FOR GODOT

BY SAMUEL BECKETT

JENNIFER BIRKETT

M

MACMILLAN
EDUCATION

First edition 1987

Published by
MACMILLAN EDUCATION LTD
Houndmills, Basingstoke, Hampshire RG21 2XS
and London
Companies and representatives
throughout the world

Printed in Hong Kong

British Library Cataloguing in Publication Data
Birkett, Jennifer
Waiting for Godot by Samuel Beckett.—
(Macmillan master guides)
1. Beckett, Samuel. En attendant Godot
I. Title
842'.914   PRQ2603.E378E6
ISBN 0–333–40865–9 Pbk
ISBN 0–333–40866–7 Pbk export

CONTENTS

GENERAL EDITOR'S PREFACE

The aim of the Macmillan Master Guides is to help you to appreciate the book you are studying by providing information about it and by suggesting ways of reading and thinking about it which will lead to a fuller understanding. The section on the writer's life and background has been designed to illustrate those aspects of the writer's life which have influenced the work, and to place it in its personal and literary context. The summaries and critical commentary are of special importance in that each brief summary of the action is followed by an examination of the significant critical points. The space which might have been given to repetitive explanatory notes has been devoted to a detailed analysis of the kind of passage which might confront you in an examination. Literary criticism is concerned with both the broader aspects of the work being studied and with its detail. The ideas which meet us in reading a great work of literature, and their relevance to us today, are an essential part of our study, and our Guides look at the thought of their subject in some detail. But just as essential is the craft with which the writer has constructed his work of art, and this may be considered under several technical headings — characterisation, language, style and stagecraft, for example.

The authors of these Guides are all teachers and writers of wide experience, and they have chosen to write about books they admire and know well in the belief that they can communicate their admiration to you. But you yourself must read and know intimately the book you are studying. No one can do that for you. You should see this book as a lamp-post. Use it to shed light, not to lean against. If you know your text and know what it is saying about life, and how it says it, then you will enjoy it, and there is no better way of passing an examination in literature.

JAMES GIBSON

ACKNOWLEDGEMENTS

Page references for *Waiting for Godot* are to the Faber Paper Covered Edition (2nd ed., 1956) and for the Trilogy are to the Picador edition (Pan Books, 1979). Critical references in the text have been reduced as far as possible; full references are given in the Bibliography. Unless otherwise stated, the dates of plays given in Chapter 1 are the dates of first production. Unless otherwise stated, translations of Beckett's work are by Beckett; other translations from the French are my own.

Cover illustration: *Two Travellers* by Jack Yeats.
Photograph © Tate Gallery Publications Department.

The author and publishers wish to thank Faber and Faber Limited for kindly granting us permission to reproduce extracts from *Waiting for Godot by Samuel Beckett*, 2nd Edition (1956).

Every effort has been made to trace all the copyright holders but if any have been inadvertently overlooked the publishers will be pleased to make the necessary arrangement at the first opportunity.

With love, for Catherine and Nathalie, who speak two languages and wait for no Godots

1 THE LIFE AND WORK OF SAMUEL BECKETT

1.1 FIRST WORDS

Samuel Beckett was born in Dublin in 1906 of respectable and well-to-do Protestant parents. His father was a quantity surveyor. His mother, a powerful and often oppressive figure, had been a nurse before her marriage and was the daughter of landed gentry. Beckett's formative years were spent in placid middle-class suburbia, fringed by the poverty and armed politics among which the Irish Republic struggled violently to birth. According to his biographer, Deirdre Bair, little of the tumult reached him personally. But in 1916, he watched the flames of the Easter Uprising from a hill outside Dublin, with his father, and 'spoke of it with fear and horror more than sixty years later'. This was the occasion when the Nationalists of the Irish Republican Army seized a number of key installations in Dublin and held them for several days against British troops. The event and the subsequent execution of the ringleaders by the British Government, which occasioned Yeats' famous poem 'Easter 1916', led to a surge of public sympathy for the Nationalist cause and made an independent Ireland inevitable.

Beckett may have been only a schoolboy at the time, but history is no respecter of age. Tumultuous and terrifying changes were taking place around him: the Uprising, the electoral victory of Sinn Fein in 1918 and Eamonn de Valera's elevation to President of the Republic, the establishment of Home Rule in 1921 and the proclamation in 1922 of the Irish Free State, followed by civil war between two wings of the Nationalist movement. The World War of 1914–18 and the Russian Revolution of 1917 would have their importance in reshaping the world in which he grew up, but for the time being their effects were further from home.

He entered Trinity College Dublin in 1923, where he read Modern Languages. He frequented the respectable salons of Anglo-Irish academics and intellectuals, discovered modern French poetry, and enjoyed the experimental European drama (especially the work of Luigi Pirandello) staged at the Gate Theatre. But he was also often to be found at the Abbey Theatre, home of Irish realism, watching Sean O'Casey's first nights, or enjoying vaudeville and popular melodrama at the Queen's Theatre, or at the new and rapidly developing popular cinema. Most of all, he learned to know Dublin's bars and pubs, drinking in a different style of culture and another kind of politics.

His work is shaped by that early experience of a society made of violent contradictions and of layers of oppression and repression. The harsh realities of life as a dependency of declining British Empire were only thinly hidden by the gloss of Anglo-Irish culture. Censorious, authoritarian churches stifled independent thought. Beckett is frank: 'I didn't like living in Ireland. You know the kind of thing, theocracy, censorship of books, that kind of thing' (Bair, p.269). Caught in the cross-fire of Protestantism and Catholicism, poverty and wealth, nationalism and internationalism, Beckett was hard put to it to find his own place. The powerless Protestant spectator of internecine Catholic violence, the situation of Vladimir and Estragon was very much his own – spotlit, isolated, apparently at the centre of a world, but knowing he was really at the edges, and unable to make sense of all its complex, shifting forces, all clamouring to take command of the world in which he lived.

This early formative experience was reinforced by that of the Second World War that came before the writing of his most important works. In 1928, with a post of *lecteur* at the Ecole Normale, Beckett had escaped from Dublin to Paris and started to carve out a career. Paris in the thirties boasted a brilliant, cosmopolitan *avant-garde*: poor but influential young Frenchmen, even poorer young Irish exiles (gravitating around James Joyce, whose close companion Beckett became), a mixed bag of male and female American writers and a mostly female collection of wealthy American patrons. Beckett began by publishing an essay on Joyce ('Dante . . . Bruno. Vico . . .Joyce') in the celebrated collection *Our Exagmination Round His Factification for Incamination of Work in Progress* (1929), alongside contributors such as William Carlos Williams and Eugène Jolas. In 1931, he published the essay on *Proust* that assured him of a lecturing job back in Trinity College (which he held 1930–31 and then gave up, to the students' relief as well as his own. In 1960, Trinity College re-incorporated him into the fold with an honorary D.Litt.) He composed his prize-winning poem *Whoroscope* (1930); he wrote other, shorter poems; he engaged in translations of poetry from the French which brought in much-needed cash: Rimbaud's 'Le Bateau ivre' and the work of the surrealists Paul Eluard, André Breton, René Crevel (1932). His first collection of short stories, *More Pricks than Kicks* was published (1934) but had no success. Nor did his first novel, *Murphy*, begun in 1934, and published in 1938. He started a play about Samuel Johnson but did not finish it.

These were small beginnings, but even so, Beckett had found his proper place and people. Only poverty and the demands of his mother drove him back on visits to Ireland. In Dublin when war was declared, he went back at once to his friends in Paris, and with them he lived through the destruction of another culture by another kind of totalitarianism. This time, however, he knew where he stood and could express his opposition. By the end of October 1940, horrified by Nazi treatment of the Jews and wanting, he said, to defend his friends, he was part of the Resistance movement in occupied Paris. He stayed in the movement until 1943 and after the war was involved through the Red Cross in some of the hard labour of the reconstruction of France. He was awarded the Croix de Guerre and the Médaille de la Résistance.

He accepted both, as he accepted in 1969 the Nobel Prize for Literature. Unlike Sartre, who refused the Prize because he felt it drafted him into the middle-class society and culture he loathed, Beckett saw, and sees, no virtue in political gestures. As will be seen later, he takes the same attitude in his writing. His aim is to make images of what is, to recreate a situation for inspection, not to press others to take sides.

In May 1946 he took up permanent residence in Paris. He had written one last novel in English, *Watt*, during the war (about 1943; pub. 1953). This is a comic investigation into the 'pursuit of meaning' which is the central theme of Beckett's work. Like Vladimir, Watt ties himself into grotesque knots in the futile attempt to make sense of a world which, Beckett believes, is a painfully and gloriously senseless game:

Watt could not accept [events] for what they perhaps were, the simple games that time plays with space, now with these toys and now with those, but was obliged, because of his peculiar character, to enquire into what they meant; oh not into what they really meant, his character was not so peculiar as all that, but into what they might be induced to mean, with the help of a little patience, a little ingenuity.

He now turned to writing in French and in the next few years produced some of his major work. Ann Beer has suggested ways in which his bilingualism has helped shape his writing and thought. It has sharpened his awareness of how *relative* to truth languages are, 'each one', she says, 'distorting and omitting parts of the unspeakable truth according to its own history and character'. As all translators know, there are some things English 'can' say that French, for example, simply 'can't', and the other way round. (Given the problem, it is amazing how little Beckett himself lost when he translated *Godot* into English. Apart from the inevitable couple of puns, the differences are remarkably slight.) But the translation problem is only a minor aspect of something even bigger, which is language's crucial inability to convey anything that even approximates to the 'real' truth of the world in and about us. Beer talks of Beckett's 'disbelief' in language:

This disbelief . . . extends to language's capacity to say anything at all about the realms beyond human consciousness – the brain's inner life, the worlds before the womb and after the grave, the origins of speech, and what lies beyond the stars.

Asked why, then, anyone should go on writing, his reply was practical: words, inadequate as they are, are all we have. The important thing is to be aware of the inadequacy and artificiality of language. A long-term resident in his adopted country, Beckett has relaxed into its language and the culture it carries, and speaks and writes it just as fluently as what we inaccurately term his 'native' tongue. (No-one is born with a language; all language is absorbed by learning.) But there is always the slight distance that comes from having made a conscious effort to learn new linguistic patterns, and it is distance that makes possible that vital, critical, detachment from the language of habit.

In July 1946, he began a novel, *Mercier et Camier*, presenting a couple whose desultory journey round and then out of a city into a desolate waste, in pursuit of a vague goal, accompanied by desultory dialogue, foreshadows the pointless activity of *Waiting for Godot* ('Did what they were looking for exist?'. . . 'What were they looking for?'. . . 'There was no hurry'.) A play, *Eleutheria*, followed, hawked vainly round producers, and three major novels *Molloy*, *Malone meurt* (*Malone Dies*) and *L'Innommable* (*The Unnamable*), written 1948–49.

These were generally much admired by the publishers who received the manuscripts and much rejected because no-one could see a market for them. All three were finally produced by the then struggling, now prestigious Editions de Minuit, the first two in 1951 and the third in 1953. In 1959, they were published as a trilogy by John Calder. In them, from a different perspective, appear many of the themes on which is constructed *Waiting for Godot*, which Beckett was writing between October 1948 and January 1949.

In these novels as in *Godot*, different characters enact different versions of Beckett's own obsession, which is to enquire into the human condition: what it is, and whether, and how, it might be different. What he is especially interested in is how the subject sees itself, what it wants, and how it is placed in the world that has made it what it is.

I use the word 'subject' carefully, in preference to 'individual', which some readers may feel would have done quite as well. It certainly comes more easily to us all in this kind of context, because it is the word we have learned to say. For that very reason, it will not do for discussing the work of a writer like Beckett, whose notions of what people are, why they are, and what they can do, go right against the grain of what we have learned.

'Individual' comes hung about with a whole baggage of assumptions and prejudices that speakers are not generally aware of. It belongs to what might be called the heroic tradition of Western culture. 'Individuals' are assumed to have a sense of themselves, to know roughly who they are and what they want, to use language freely to express themselves, to have minds of their own. They are or ought to be free to do what they choose.

In Beckett's book, no such beast exists – though there are several, like Vladimir and Estragon, who think of themselves in that style. For Beckett, human being is split. It is certainly the subject 'I', who seems to dominate the action, as in the grammar book distinction 'subject–verb–object'. But it is also passive, subject-ed, depending for its whole existence on other agents and higher authorities. It is also, then, a subject in the very different sense in which we are subjects of Kings, Queens or States.

Chiefly, for Beckett, what subjects are subject-ed to is language. We don't speak to 'express' ourselves. When we speak, we simply give back learned language. Our sense of self is structured, constituted and invented by language. We are the speech we learn from our mothers, our families and our culture. This speech involves not just words but the grammatical structures that put words into relationships with each other, and the structures and patterns by which we 'think' (that is, marshal, drill and organise our arguments), and beyond them the structures and patterns by which society is organised. Consider the way Vladimir builds up arguments to persuade and bully Estragon into agreeing that the place they are is the place they were yesterday, and that this is the place of an appointment with Godot. And then consider how similar his style is to the way Pozzo persuades, seduces and bullies the couple into agreeing to stick around and be his audience. The instruments of power vary but the patterns are the same. Pozzo's whip is simply more visible.

Language produces the human speaker and not the other way round. And whether we look for our identity in the past or in the future, hoping all the time to find something different, we never find anything but the same patterns as we are living through in the present. This is what the novel trilogy explores. The kind of awareness it makes available to Beckett, and to us, is not, you will realise, granted to the characters who figure in *Godot*. It is because they do not understand the limits on and in them that their actions and language are so hollow, and their frenzied attempts to fix a meaning for themselves are so tragically futile.

The first two parts of the trilogy present images of the silence and speech between which, for Beckett, human being oscillates. On the one hand is the desire to be silent, to be rid of all the corruptions of learned language. On the other, there is the desire to speak forever, to try out all the languages of Babel in the hope of randomly releasing something unexpected from which a new start can be made. The third part puts both options together to give a total vision of what the new might be: something beyond the grasp of present speech, quite unnamable – for if it could be named in existing language, it wouldn't be new.

Molloy is trying to get back to silence. He is on a quest for the point of his beginning, an attempt to get back to his mother. This is another version of Vladimir and Estragon's quest for the point of ending, which they call being with Godot. Both quests are pointless, because past and future are equally beyond our knowing. All that we ever know is the present. (And in another sense, we cannot know the present. We can only experience it without analysing it; once we try to pin it down with a description, it becomes past.)

The desire to 'get back to the womb', 'back to nature', or 'back to the pure self', uncorrupted by what Beckett calls the voices from outside, is one of the many delusions our culture has sold us. This desire, which we might call the 'myth of origins', is as much of a trap as the dream of Godot. Molloy knows dimly he's on a hiding to nothing, but something in the way he's made pushes him to carry on.

His search is futile because all he can ever see is what he is. When he gets to the place where he thought his mother was, she is dead. Where he had expected to find her, he finds himself: 'I have her room. I sleep in her bed. I piss and shit in her pot. I have taken her place. I must resemble her more and more' (p.9). The self he finds is the one he shares with his mother, and with the culture that she handed on to him. It stinks of rot and decay and can say nothing he doesn't already know. Molloy's old mother is closely related to the Boy sent by Godot, whose answers to questions are all shaped by the data that the questions program in.

Like Vladimir and Estragon, Molloy establishes that you get nowhere new if you are hampered by the old rubbish. He establishes too how near-impossible it is to be free of the rubbish, and how many diversions and distractions tempt the seeker from his path. Molloy condemns diversions, especially that prime diversion, suicide: 'Backsliding has always depressed me, but life seems made up of backsliding, and death itself must be a kind of backsliding' (p.57). In contrast, Vladimir and Estragon devote their whole lives to them.

Molloy, unlike the later pair, is rescued. For the second half of his book, Beckett finds another self-projection, Moran, and briefs him to try and find Molloy. Like the second act of *Waiting for Godot*, this re-run is a second chance, an opportunity to do something different. Unlike Vladimir and Estragon, Molloy seizes the chance, and the result is the start of a new way of living, which begins with a new kind of language. The key to the grammar of the new language is the recognition that words tell nothing of reality. This is why Moran's report begins as it does, with what is now one of the most-quoted examples of the new writing:

> I went back into the house and wrote, It is midnight. The rain is beating on the windows. It was not midnight. It was not raining. (p.162)

Whether or not he found Molloy doesn't matter. It isn't having found, but the process of seeking that is important; not possessing a dead truth, but creating a new language for a new life. Life isn't a fixed goal but a fluid present.

Malone Dies not in silence but with a flourish of speech. Malone, on his deathbed, has no intention of finishing. Instead, he 'plays', planning to recall characters and stories out of his own brain and when they're gone to 'make an inventory' of the objects in his possession. (Vladimir and Estragon work in the same way. Godot is almost the only character they can recall to tell stories about, but they do their best with objects: tree, hat and boots.) What happens as Malone plays, making lots of new tales – though still in the old patterns – is that suddenly the old rubbish does indeed disappear, and a new character (Macmann) emerges.

Macmann is a deliberately ludicrous image of the desire for a new world, and his comic nature shows how impossible such a dream must appear. Indeed, a sudden twist of the text places Macmann in the lunatic asylum. There, like Vladimir and Estragon, he keeps his head down, play-acting escape, hating and yet loving the keepers who beat him and feed him, afraid to leave the safety of the high walls of the institution for the unknown open road.

Yet Macmann's tale ends with a fantasy of freedom. Unexpectedly, the lunatics take over the asylum, killing their keepers in an act of black comic violence. This is, of course, nothing more than the dream of the dying narrator, Malone, but this dream makes an important, subversive and optimistic statement. The powers and conventions that keep us intellectually and physically in line are foolish and fragile and vulnerable to attack. Sheer chance may suddenly give opportunities, of which something might come. The point is not to backslide but to hold on and keep playing, no matter how ludicrous the enterprise becomes:

> I shall never do anything any more from now on but play . . . perhaps I shall not succeed any better than hitherto. Perhaps as hitherto I shall find myself abandoned, in the dark, without anything to play with. Then I shall play with myself. To have been able to conceive such a plan is encouraging. (p.166)

The third part of the trilogy, *The Unnamable*, sets speech and silence against each other to blow wide open the notion of meaning. The first line of the novel is a shorthand version of the whole process:

> Where now? Who now? When now? Unquestioning. I, say I. Unbelieving.

Asking questions is not enough. The opposite – not asking questions, or else making statements – is not enough either. Somewhere else – somewhere in between – is where 'I' want to be. Though I shall never really be; all I can do is 'say'.

Vladmir and Estragon ask questions and they make statements. But they do so as though they expect to get answers or to establish facts. So all they ever do is pass the time with their words. To get anywhere, they would have to make that quantum jump of realisation that the words we have never really 'mean', only ever 'say'.

The unnamed 'I' who speaks in this novel – yet another of Beckett's self-projections – reviews the characters he has so far invented, who have dramatised for him the conventions that beset his (and our) being, the foolish illusions by which we live: believing in the importance of origins, believing in God, believing that man is rational, humane and benevolent. Vladimir and Estragon are not mentioned in the roll-call, but they too live by these delusions, which 'I' dismisses as 'rubbish': 'Some of this rubbish has come in handy on occasions, I don't deny it . . . I use it still, to scratch my arse with' (p.273).

Abandoning all his old characters, the speaker finds a new one, Worm, who is not just ludicrous, like Macmann, but grotesque to the point of repulsiveness. Worm is not human by any known definition. This is an advantage. He has no eyes, ears, or sexual organs, no orifices though which the taught responses of the outside world can get in. All he has is a mouth, ready to make an authentic utterance – and, alas, incapable of uttering, because without the words convention teaches, how can anyone speak?

Worm is the threshold of new meaning where Beckett's writing is always forced to end. He is the point at which there is awareness of the limits of language coupled with the acknowledgement that without the use of the corrupt organs of knowledge and speech no new words can be born.

Worm is something of an abortion. It might have been better not to try to give him life: 'some people are lucky', he says, 'born of a wet dream and dead before morning' (p.349). But at least he knows, and resents, that he is not what he wanted to be, which was 'something quite different . . . not like it, like me, in my own way' (p.356).

Worm collapses in a frenzy of frustration and the 'orator' takes charge. This is the same jauntily self-confident 'I' as is played by Pozzo, who fears change and renewal and doesn't care how decayed the world is, as long as he can rule it. Juggling every cliché in the book, he puts the elements of the old universe together in the old familiar, habitual order, with all the old, familiar, habitual lies. He reinstates life's hell, and calls it paradise:

Unusual hell when you come to think of it, perhaps it's paradise . . . you scarcely breathe, but you breathe . . . not so blind as all that my eyes, they're not mine, mine are done, they don't even weep any more, they open and shut by the force or habit. (p.361)

The Unnamable suggests two alternatives. Either 'I' must write a joyful revolution in speaking and being, even though the basic materials – new words – are not there. Or else 'I' must stop my struggles to be 'me' and give in to the old voices of authority and convention. In this text, it is obvious that the first option is the one that 'I' and Beckett prefer. In *Waiting for Godot*, it is an option that is never considered. Granted every day the chance and the materials of a new start, Vladimir and Estragon cling doggedly to old patterns, old habits, and old masters.

1.2 WAITING FOR GODOT

In the spring of 1950 the manuscripts of *Waiting for Godot* and Beckett's earlier play, *Eleutheria*, reached Roger Blin, a friend of Artaud, who at the time was directing Strindberg's *Ghost Sonata* at the Gaité-Montparnasse. Blin liked both, but opted in the end for *Godot* because it would cost less to stage. 'I was poor', he told Deirdre Bair, 'I didn't have a penny. . . . there were only four actors and they were bums. They could wear their own clothes if it came to that, and I wouldn't need anything but a spotlight and a bare branch for a tree' (Bair, p.403). A grant from the French Ministry of Arts and Letters bridged the remaining gaps. There were still problems. Actors were reluctant to commit themselves to what looked like being a very short run. Several who began rehearsal soon left, unable to understand their parts or learn the lines. Finding a suitable theatre was also a headache, but eventually the Théâtre de Babylone was made available.

Blin suggested some cuts, which Beckett later incorporated into his English translation. Beckett discussed the staging with Blin and attended rehearsals but largely limited his contribution to quiet deflection of some of Blin's more elaborate ideas, such as turning the whole performance into a circus. In the end, the circus mood was to some extent retained but the production was kept very simple. The opening night (January 1953), which Beckett did not attend, was a *succès de scandale*.

A second production by Blin in September 1953 at the same theatre preceded a European tour. Censorship slowed down the transfer of the play to London, but eventually Peter Hall staged the play at the Arts Theatre Club, 3 August 1955. The first night was badly received by the popular press, but reviews by Kenneth Tynan and Harold Hobson in the *Observer* and *Sunday Times* respectively (7 August) turned the tide. From September 1955 to May 1956, the play played to capacity audiences at the Criterion Theatre. An upopular try-out in Miami (January 1956) with the popular comedian Bert Lahr, who had played the lion in *The Wizard of Oz*, unwisely advertised as 'the laugh sensation of two continents', was recouped by a successful version in New York in April. An all-black cast performed the play on Broadway in January 1957.

A list of other productions must include Alan Simpson's first Irish production (Pike Theatre, Dublin, 1955), a production at San Quentin prison, California, November 1957, Blin's revival at the Odéon, Paris (spring 1961), Anthony Page's production at the Royal Court (winter 1964-65) and the Schiller Theater version (1975), directed by Beckett himself. In 1978, the Comédie Française took the play into their repertory. The BBC first broadcast it on television in 1961 (it scored a very low 32 on the BBC Reaction Index) and on the Third Programme in April 1960. The French text was published in October 1952, Beckett's English translation in New York in 1954, and the definitive version in 1965. Translations and requests for permission to stage the play were countless. Beckett's work continued to be seen as difficult, but his reputation was assured.

1.3 SUBSEQUENT STORIES

A brief run through Beckett's work after *Godot* shows the same themes taken up in different versions and from different perspectives. It is not a question of his ideas being developed in the traditional sense – worked out to the point of perfection and completion – but of his vision being expanded and elaborated through more and more 'delegates', in a never-ending sequence of never-ending stories. Like Lucky's speech, his writing takes the same patterns through a series of different forms, and as it nears its end (Beckett's own death, still in the future) it becomes shorter, and its terms more sparse.

Beckett's next stage play, *Fin de partie* (*Endgame*), was directed by Roger Blin and staged first at the Royal Court and then in Paris (April 1957). In this crueller, more hopeless version of the limited world of decaying language and culture explored in *Godot*, blind Hamm, confined to his wheelchair and four grey walls, is the sole possessor of the key to the food cupboard. He beguiles his endless declining days with petty vengeances on his legless parents, dying in dustbins behind him, sadistic fantasies of supplicants who vainly beseech his benevolence, and calculated cruelty to his servant, Clov, whose dreams of new life are forever confined by the dismal language of the old world that Hamm has taught him. A more articulate version of Estragon, Clov bitterly attacks Hamm's obsession with 'yesterday':

What does that mean? Yesterday! That means that bloody awful day, long ago, before this bloody awful day. I use the words you taught me. If they don't mean anything any more, teach me others. Or let me·be silent.

Krapp's Last Tape (1958), the next play for the stage, presents an old man who for years has been re-running the taped record of his life, constantly 'embarking on a new retrospect' until it becomes 'clear to me at last that the dark I have always struggled to keep under is in reality my most [break]'. It is left unclear whether the dark unknown in himself and the world outside is something valuable or something to be feared, but the evidence seems to weigh down on the side of the first. The Vladimir who runs over quietly to himself, at the end of *Godot*, the events of his last two days, finding as he looks back new interpretations of what he has been, is rather like a Krapp at the start of his tape-running project. Unlike *Godot*, this play speaks optim-istically of the possibilities of change in the most rigid characters. 'Just been listening,' Krapp snorts, 'to that stupid bastard I took myself for thirty years ago, hard to believe I was ever as bad as all that'.

In *Happy Days* (1961), Winnie, buried deep in sand to her waist and then her neck, is as clear an image of near-unchanging near-immobility as Vladimir and Estragon. Like them, she alternates between struggling and waiting, her only consolation that Willie (she thinks) is probably listening to her monologue: 'Something of this is being heard, I am not merely talking to myself'. This is even wilder black humour than *Godot*, with Winnie laughing and screaming, trying to remember 'that wonderful line "laughing wild amid severest woe"'. She, too, lives on words and memories and the dream of two kinds of happy days: the death that is to come ('the happy day to come when flesh melts at so many degrees and the night of the moon has so many hundred hours') and the rare days when Willie speaks. But pinning her hopes on Willie is not as foolish as pinning them on Godot. He is a real person, her husband, on stage beside her, and on this particular day not only listening but speaking, and even bursting into song. At the last moment, in the last scene, after years, apparently, of keeping his distance, he climbs up the heap of sand and the curtain falls as the two faces confront each other, motionless. What will happen could be nothing, or something wholly new – a kiss, an insult, or something else – and so beyond our knowing and beyond the drama's power to say. But it is a possibility of change, which in *Godot* is not sketched at all.

The man and two women, husband, wife and mistress, obsessively recounting an old adultery in *Play* (1963), are up to the neck in urns, speaking only as the erratic play of the spotlight falls on their faces. This is a stark image of the isolation, vulnerability and passivity of human speakers, who have no power to speak of their own free will, no assurance of a world out there to speak to, and no assurance of being understood. It helps us understand why, if Godot did not exist, we could be strongly tempted to invent him.

'Breath' (1970), a 120-word 35-second scene of light and breathing, is drama at the vanishing point, the absolute minimum of light and sound. It was written at the request of Kenneth Tynan for his show *Oh! Calcutta!*, without Beckett realising what kind of a show Tynan had in mind. He was irritated to find his text tampered with and his minimum, as it were, maximised, so that a stage scattered with rubbish became a stage scattered with rubbish and naked bodies.

A play specially written for television, *Eh Joe* (1966), shows the struggle not to be: a silent Joe trying to silence the voices of his memories, 'Throttling the dead in his head'. *Not I* (1972) presents the reverse: a mouth, belonging to an old woman, speaking its life away in a 15-minute monologue, faster and faster as it nears the end and all the time trying desperately to avoid confronting the pain of self-knowledge, never saying 'I', always dodging away into 'she', pretending 'I' is someone else.

That Time (1976) presents an old man with tape recordings of his own past voices. *Footfalls* (1976) and *Ghost Trio* (1977), turn to movement and silence and away from words.

Beckett has also experimented with radio plays: *All that Fall* (1956); *Embers* (1959); *Words and Music* (1962); *Cascando* (1963). His screenplay for the silent *Film* (1965), starring Buster Keaton, dramatises yet again the impossibility of perceiving and knowing the human subject, and the fact that all that is ever known is oneself. Chased down streets and alleys, caught at last inside his own room, Keaton is finally fixed by the camera's eye, which turns out to be his own, and ends frozen in pitiless, frightening and completely impenetrable scrutiny of himself.

In the sixties and seventies, Beckett also produced short prose texts and a kind of novel, *Comment c'est* (*How it is*), (1961), which is an important experiment in finding 'a form that accommodates the mess' (Beckett, cit. Bair, p.523). Against conventional writing that tries to order, repress and suppress the impenetrable confusion of reality, Beckett tries to let the confusion find its own voice, or rather, voices, for truth is not one and indivisible but many, and all unspeakable. The best ending for this section – and not a bad introduction to *Godot* – is Beckett's own characterisation of the form of his work, which he offered to Harold Pinter:

> If you insist on finding form, I'll describe it for you. I was in hospital once. There was a man in another ward, dying of throat cancer. In the silence, I could hear his screams continually. That's the only kind of form my work has. (cit. Bair, p.528)

2 SUMMARY
AND CRITICAL COMMENTARY

The play consists of two near-symmetrical acts, each of which covers the events of two evenings between twilight and nightfall. The place is the same in both: a country road, with a tree (bare in Act 1, but with 'four or five leaves' in Act 2) and a mound.

The second act is a little shorter than the first. In the German production Beckett directed in 1975, Act 1 ran for 70 minutes and Act 2 for 55. Both contain three similar blocks of action. Vladimir and Estragon, a near-destitute couple of whose origins we know nothing, are reunited after a night spent apart and engage in a variety of activities to pass the time while waiting for a certain Godot, with whom they think they have an appointment. Another couple, Pozzo and Lucky, pass by and stop briefly. After they leave, the friends look for more diversions to pass the time until a messenger boy arrives, who says Godot has sent him to say he cannot make the appointment but will be along the next day.

Vivian Mercier's joke synopsis of the play – one in which nothing happens, twice – is not entirely wrong. Anyone who buys a ticket expecting to see conventional, self-assured heroes acting out conventional dilemmas and dramas on the well-decorated stage of the world of our familiar complexities will not see very much. But from the perspective of a couple living on the margins of society, reduced for survival to a minimum of experience and expectations, a great deal is going on. Between them, picking over the scanty leavings of someone else's scrap-heap, Vladimir and Estragon root out ways of constructing sense out of an inherently senseless universe. Within their limits, they do as much as they can, and the audience, drawn into an understanding of the effort required for such minimal achievements, recognises a new kind of heroism, whose failures are comic as well as tragic. What happens is not nothing, but the generation between stage and audience of tremendous dramatic emotion: a sense of admiration, amusement, irritation, sympathy and above all frustration at and on behalf of characters trapped in the grotesque, making the best of futility.

What also happens is that that frustration pushes the audience into fresh perceptions that the characters on stage cannot reach, being too deep into the muck-heap to see clearly. The audience glimpses the limitations of those ways of living of which Vladimir and Estragon get just the bones. (Their better-endowed fellow-citizens still get enough meat off them for their usefulness not to be questioned.) For the audience, the banal exchanges between the characters on stage take on another dimension of meaning. The nothing that is demonstrated twice on stage is the underlying bankruptcy of European civilization.

ACT 1

First block: the couple passing time

Doing nothing
The action begins with Estragon sitting on the mound, struggling to take off his boot. Vladimir enters 'advancing with short, stiff strides, legs wide apart'. Estragon's sore feet and Vladimir's bladder problems between them shape this opening visual image of action and movement which is difficult and painful and yet, with unwitting heroism, persevered with. Between them, they present the double nature of the human condition as Beckett sees it. In Estragon, it is the urge to get rid of the constraints and pinches of culture and to move back to silence; in Vladimir, the urge to continue within and despite the constraints, perpetually producing speech.

Their first spoken exchange echoes this. Estragon, giving up on his boot, remarks 'Nothing to be done'. Vladimir is almost ready to agree, though in the past he has always 'resumed the struggle'. At the end of this short sequence, he too concedes: 'Nothing to be done'. The original French is more ambiguous. 'Rien à faire' could be 'Nothing doing', 'Nothing to do' or 'Nothing to be done'. Beckett's English translation insists on the latter. Putting the verb – the action word – into the passive form emphasises again that double urge to act and to give in, to speak and to surrender to silence.

Some critics have pointed out in that 'Nothing to be done' the echo of Lenin's famous revolutionary pamphlet ('What is to be done?') and have coupled with that the echo of a famous 1930s' agitprop play about socialist Utopia, Clifford Odets' *Waiting for Lefty*. One implication would be that the blindness of Beckett's tramps to their real condition is a major obstacle to change. Ruby Cohn has seen an echo of another kind, of the great clown Grock's resigned catchphrase, 'Nicht mööööglich' – ' It's not poooossible' (*Just Play*, p.12). There is no need to choose between the echoes. All these fragments are part of the massive inheritance of leftovers out of which some substance has to be concocted.

This first exchange is a negative one, with much pain and rejection and very little sympathy. The characters demonstrate none of the profound and complex feelings that we have been taught are an innate human characteristic (and which Worm's inventor has already told us simply don't exist). Estragon is just not interested in Vladimir's dramatic offer of an embrace to celebrate their reunion. The fact that he's spent the night in a ditch, and 'they' beat him again, is to him just a fact of life. Far more pressing to him is the pain of his feet, which blinds him to all other concerns. It is equalled only by the pain of Vladimir's bladder which deafens him to Estragon's calls for help.

The two thieves

As Estragon, boot off at last, airs his toes, Vladimir starts up a fresh and unexpectedly deep line of thought. He offers his unwilling listener the story of the two thieves in the Gospels, crucified alongside Christ, one supposedly saved and the other damned. This is 'a reasonable percentage', he thinks, and he suggests they divert themselves for a time with repenting. But as Estragon points out, they have nothing to repent, except possibly 'Our being born'. Estragon's down-to-earth approach makes him something of a spoil-sport for a friend who passes his time inventing fantasy versions of real problems, but his stubborn clinging to material fact gets him closer to truth than Vladimir. As his comment implies, it is living that produces pain and suffering, not sin, which is the theologians' invention. Finally he silences Vladimir's craving to be conned in the only way possible, with a crude insult: 'People are bloody ignorant apes'. In the insult, there is a witty double-take with the reference to Darwin's thesis that men are evolved from apes, not created by God in the garden of Eden. Only an ape, says Darwin's ape, could swallow this Christian twaddle.

Coming just before the first mention of Godot, this exchange suggests some connection in Vladimir's mind between what Christianity offers and what his God-fantasy involves: rescue, refuge and a strong authority to take over his moral responsibilities.

The appointment with Godot

Estragon makes the sensible suggestion that they leave this unprepossessing spot. Vladimir says they can't, because they're waiting for Godot. This is the beginning of the day's process of tying themselves down to futile anticipation. It has however the short-term advantage of provoking a machine-gun burst of conversation. Estragon, resisting incorporation into Vladimir's wish-fulfilments, insinuates that this isn't the right tree, the right place, or even the right day, cruelly winding up Vladimir to a hysterical panic of uncertainty. The exchange exhausts them both. Estragon immediately falls asleep and is woken by Vladimir, frightened to be left alone. With his own kind of cruelty, Vladimir refuses to soothe Estragon's fears by sharing his nightmares. There is the prospect of a quarrel and Estragon threatens to leave. All is resolved with a grandiose embrace – undercut by a crude music-hall double-take: '[Estragon recoils.] You stink of garlic!'

Playing hanging

This is Estragon's suggestion, an exciting prospect in more senses than one. However, a debate about the mechanics of the game and the strength of the branches leads them to an indisputably correct decision: 'Don't let's do anything. It's safer'.

Their alternative to suicide is talking about Godot. He is now assumed to be definitely coming; the more they discuss him, the more real he gets. 'What exactly did we ask him for?' asks Estragon. The result is an echo word-game of variations on Vladimir's imprecise response: 'Nothing very definite'. In this strange cross-talk sequence (p.18), concrete nouns are undermined by qualifications ('a kind of prayer' . . . 'a vague supplication') and a firm past tense ('What did we ask for?') replaced by conditionals ('he'd see' . . .' 'he couldn't promise' . . . 'he'd have to think it over'). An effect of hollowness is created; these are statements with no hard centre to them. Estragon's triumph is to turn this dreamed-up Godot into a man with a conventional businessman's history, the owner of a 'home', totally preoccupied with their request, consulting 'his friends', 'his books', 'his bank account'. 'It's the normal thing' they conclude, finally turning their invention into reality.

The consequences are immediate and unpleasant. They now have to bow down before this authority of their own making:

ESTRAGON: [anxious] And we? . . . Where do we come in? . . .
VLADIMIR: Come in? On our hands and knees.

By tying themselves down to a pattern of dependence, they have lost all their rights, including the right to freedom. As Vladimir says, distinctly, 'We got rid of them'. With this realisation, fear enters the drama for the first time, and it is fear of their own invention.

The carrot

Humans are good at displacing and repressing their fears. Estragon displaces his with the traditional call for consolation ('I'm hungry') and Vladimir promptly distracts him with a carrot. The ploy emphasises the ludicrous gap between the greatness of the terrors that people are faced with and the ease with which they accept dummy comforters.

At least Estragon is not totally satisfied by the carrot: 'Funny, the more you eat the worse it gets'. Vladimir is more ready to take what is offered: 'I get used to the muck as I go along'. They react in similar ways to the figure of Godot, produced to stave off Vladimir's hunger for certainty. Estragon resists it, with suspicion, while Vladimir swallows everything, despite its increasing unpleasantness. He will shortly tell Pozzo that Godot is a 'kind of acquaintance', indignantly opposed by Estragon: 'Nothing of the kind, we hardly know him' (p.23).

Second block: Pozzo and Lucky

A frightening cry off-stage, reducing Vladimir and Estragon to jelly, heralds the appearance of Lucky, bowed under Pozzo's baggage, with a long rope round his neck whose end is held by the whip-cracking Pozzo. Their first fear is that this is Godot. It is not, but his arrogance, proprietorial condescension and cruelty make the two of them hard, as Estragon says, to tell apart in the half-light. The structural links between capitalism and authoritarian versions of religious faith are clearly hinted.

Pozzo may seem self-sufficient (if we forget Lucky, as is easily done) but he is glad of an audience. Vladimir and Estragon are ready to be cast as admirers and dependants, which is the role they have already adopted in relation to Godot. Putting on his coat, taking up his whip, sitting on his stool, opening up his basket and gnawing on his chicken, Pozzo emphasises his possessions and his self-possession, in stark contrast to their total lack.

Interestingly, the friends' first attention is rather for Lucky, dropping asleep on his feet, sagging under the weight of the bags, and a horrific sore on his neck. Their response is a mixture of compassion and contempt. Pozzo intercepts their attempts to address his slave, carefully making himself the focus of attention. Vladimir neverthe-less finds in himself the courage and the language to attack the 'scandal' of this treatment of a 'man', a 'human being'. Vladimir would like to leave: 'Let's go' (p.28). This time it is Estragon who wants to stay, won over by Pozzo's gift of the bones that should have gone to Lucky. Finally Vladimir too is seduced by Pozzo's willingness to play along with his Godot fiction. It would seem that entering the Godot trap is a package deal, which involves accepting a considerable number of other unpleasantnesses as also 'normal'.

The short-term reward of collaborating with Pozzo is a wealth of conversation and story to fill the time. His audience can even share his sense that time's passing is in his control. Unfortunately, exploit-ing Lucky would seem to be the condition of such pleasures. The tramps have entered a situation which develops their considerable potential for cruelty.

They remain attached for some time to the crucial question of why Lucky doesn't put down his bags. Pozzo, like a skilled politician, dodges it as long as he can, through several reiterations and a miming and makes a meal of preparing to reply: 'Is everybody ready? Is everybody looking at me?' (p.30). His eventual answer is the politician's blend of deviousness and cynical frankness. No-one disputes Lucky's right to put them down, so presumably he does it from choice. He does it to impress and placate his owner, in the vain hope of being kept on. Pozzo has no intention of doing so and is taking him to the fair to sell him. Lucky's situation may seem unfortunate, but it pains Pozzo far more than it pains him. Finally, Pozzo points out that it's sheer chance that he is on top and Lucky underneath, and things could easily be reversed. Lucky is just unlucky.

This is a brilliant satire of the comfortable prejudice of those in power that the powerless can act from choice. In fact, like Didi and Gogo, once they have conceded their freedom they have no rights or choices left. There is a chilling intimation here of how Godot would behave, if they ever met him. As Pozzo says, there is no way that Lucky could hope to sway him, because Lucky can so easily be replaced: 'As though I were short of slaves!'

Estragon's tentative sympathy for Lucky's tears is greeted not with gratitude but a violent kick. Lucky has more sense than to kick Pozzo, so takes revenge on someone even weaker than himself. Inhumanity would seem to be the key to survival. Certainly, for the great survivor Pozzo, the tears of Lucky and Estragon are of no concern in themselves. They simply give him a pretext for a pseudo-philosophical disquisition on the weight of human suffering (p.33).

It now turns out that Pozzo's impressive rhetoric has all been learned from Lucky. A 'professional' man, of commonplace thoughts and feelings, he knew he had to buy in his values: 'Beauty, grace, truth of the first water, I knew they were beyond me. So I took a knook' (p.33). The implication is that all high culture is no more than a pretty mask on the face of capital. The word 'knook' (probably Beckett's own invention) is not explained in the English text, but in the French original, Pozzo is more forthcoming: 'Once people had jesters. Now they have knooks. Those who can afford it'. Philosophy is only a rich man's entertainment, another way of passing the time.

A series of grotesque entertainments follows, all 'Worse than the pantomime' (p.35). There is amusement for Estragon in watching Pozzo's panic as he discovers his pipe is gone. Both Estragon and Pozzo are fascinated by the sight of Vladimir peeing painfully off-stage. Pozzo becomes instructive and explains the twilight, in the bizarre jumble which is the professional man's language, a ragbag of pretentious lyricism and precise prosaicism ('after having poured forth ever since . . . say ten o'clock in the morning'), learned words and rude noises ('pppfff!', 'pop!').

Pozzo claims to have given Vladimir and Estragon a great deal: bones, talk, and an explanation of the twilight. They have given him more: attention, time, and admiration, but he's not concerned with that. As a further gift, he offers a show by Lucky which, he claims, will cost him (Pozzo) a lot of effort. Lucky performs to order. He refused once, Pozzo says ominously, but though the tramps pursue the point they never find out what happened. The unspoken threat of Pozzo's power is left hanging in the air, uncashed – and all the more potent for that.

Lucky sketches a dance, which Pozzo says he calls 'The Net. He thinks he's entangled in a net'. It is a measure of Pozzo's power that he can watch this clear representation of Lucky's plight without feeling in the least bit threatened by it. Establishment armour is barely dented by the challenge of *avant-garde* art. Lucky's weakness is stressed further by the business with his hat, a kind of on-off switch that ensures his thoughts are controlled.

Yet his tirade is still disturbing for his audience. Pozzo sits dejected and groaning throughout, while the tramps alternately listen attentively or utter protests. At the end, they are moved to violence by Lucky's hysterical insistence on 'the skull' that lurks under all life, and they roughly de-hat him. The whole speech is an encyclopaedic overview of all the shreds of untruth that Lucky and his fellow jesters in the European tradition have produced. It is punctuated by references to learned authorities, so-called guarantors of its accuracy, which are increasingly comic and obscene (Puncher and Wattmann, Testew and Cunard, Fartov and Belcher). It mixes fact and fiction, setting on the same level the 'divine Miranda' of Shakespeare's *Tempest*, the magician's daughter, and the speculative philosopher Bishop Berkeley. In the first half, three sections deal with soul, mind and body. Disjointed shreds of abstruse Christian theology and crude superstition give an impression of the inconsistency of a faith that starts with a 'personal' God and ends with the fires of hell. Intellect, reason and science are nothing more than a series of names and 'labours left unfinished'. The body too is a decaying asset, for all the cult of sport and the progress of medicine. 'Waste and pine', 'dying', 'shrink and dwindle' mark the beginning, middle and end of this section.

The second half evokes the dying and decomposition of matter and the inability of the human mind to keep control of it. Places named by humans, city and country ('Feckham Peckham Fulham Clapham', 'Connemara') give way to undefined plains, mountains, seas and rivers, which in turn break down into the basic elements (water, fire, air, earth). In the end, 'stones', 'cold', 'skull', 'grave' – death – are the obsessive images.

As distressing as Lucky's vision of death's abiding presence in life is the death of the language and logic by which that vision has been constructed. The nuts and bolts of the creaky old machine are not only showing through but coming apart. Words and phrases like 'given', 'considering', 'as a result of', 'it is established', 'beyond all doubt', 'simultaneously', all implying the ability to order, discuss and conclude, are shown to be empty and powerless. The real constants of Lucky's knowledge are few: 'for reasons unknown', 'time will tell', 'labours unfinished', 'shrink and dwindle'. In short, he knows nothing. Even the nothing he knows is ambiguous. Does 'time will tell' mean we shall have knowledge one day, or just that time will wear us out, take its toll?

This is rubbish Lucky and his like have often repeated for Pozzo and his like. As it's repeated (just like Vladimir and Estragon's repetition of their days), bits wear out and the repetitions become faster and shorter. Lucky's speech recreates the increasing momentum of subjective time as it draws to its end; the nearer death, like the nearer night, the faster life goes and the more suddenly the end comes. This is Lucky's personal experience of the panic of the human condition: 'I resume', 'in short', 'in brief', *but not so fast*.

There can be nothing left after this but departure. Though even departure is almost more than humans can manage. Even Pozzo finds it hard:

POZZO: I don't seem able . . . [long hesitation] . . . to depart.
ESTRAGON: Such is life. (p. 47)

But Pozzo can leave eventually, as long as he has Lucky and his whip to help him advance. We know he is advancing because he tells us so, and he has the whip hand: 'Up! Pig! On! Faster! On!' A world may be morally and intellectually bankrupt, but force and a sold-out intelligentsia can still keep it going.

Third block: the boy

Estragon suggests again that he and Vladimir should go too, but the routine is by now despairingly familiar. They can't go, because they're waiting for Godot. They discuss Pozzo and Lucky. Vladimir remarks how they've changed, introducing a new and totally unfounded claim that the master and his slave have been in this place before and so are part of a routine, which increases his sense of comforting familiarity with this place.

Estragon's response to Vladimir's 'How they've changed!' takes the platitude and twists it into a bitterly profound comment: 'They all change. Only we can't'. They can't, because they're fixed by waiting for Godot.

The timid entrance of the Boy introduces a sequence which re-enacts the relationship between self and outside world. All people can ever see in the world outside them is another version of their own knowledge and perceptions. The information that comes back is the same as the information that is fed in. A great deal of input may sometimes generate a little extra unfamiliar information, but it all still takes the shape of the original data. If the Boy is the unknown future for which Vladimir and Estragon are longing, then he is a future constructed in their own image.

He begins by addressing Vladimir as Mister Albert. Vladimir accepts the name; he takes what comes, whether it is meant for him or not. Estragon's is a rough approach. He asks the Boy simple questions, with no prompts in them ('What do you want?', 'What kept you so late?') and so he gets no answers. Vladimir speaks kindly, feeding him lines and getting back exactly the answers he wants: 'You

---

don't know me?'–'No, sir'; 'It wasn't you came yesterday?'–'No, sir'; 'This is your first time?'–'Yes, sir'. When Vladimir clearly commands: 'Speak', the Boy pours out a flood of words which give nothing more than what the couple have already themselves conjectured: 'Mr Godot told me to tell you he won't come this evening but surely tomorrow'. Godot certainly exists as words, in the form of the message, but whether he is anything more is still uncertain. There is a nice ambiguity in the Boy's 'surely'.

Vladimir elicts further information, which seems fresh but is not; it is simply a variation on themes he and Estragon have already discussed. The Boy has a brother, not unlike him, and they both work for Godot. One is beaten and the other is not – echoing the different overnight fates of Estragon and Vladimir and also the fate of the two crucified thieves, one saved and one damned. One boy minds the sheep and the other the goats: another religious echo of judgement. Justice and love don't seem to come into Godot's arbitrary beatings, and this again tallies exactly with the couple's own experience. There is no more certainty in the 'refuge' with Godot than in their existing present:

VLADIMIR: You don't know if you're unhappy or not?
BOY: No, sir
VLADIMIR: You're as bad as myself. (p.51)

The boy leaves, night falls and the moon rises, releasing them from their wait. Estragon abandons his boots. Vladimir assures him Godot will come the next day; Estragon is more minded to return with a rope. Ironically, as the day ends they seem to take on a new life. Even Estragon starts remembering. But it's only a last flare of routine, and the vigour is short-lived. They think briefly of parting, but it's much too late for a new start. 'It's not worth while' to part now, nor indeed to move at all. The curtain falls on a point which is neither coming, nor going, as near full stop as is possible without being dead:

ESTRAGON: Well, shall we go?
VLADIMIR: Yes, let's go.
                                        [They do not move.]

Compared with the melodramatic flurry of movement which was Pozzo and Lucky's exit, this seems almost a confession of complete defeat. But it is not. We do not see them ending; what they do next is out of our perception.

ACT 2

First block: the couple passing time

Time and place are exactly the same, except that Estragon's boots occupy the centre stage, with Lucky's hat, and the tree has four or five leaves. Vladimir enters alone and notices the tree. It clearly upsets him, being a change of which he has had no previous experience. But he has dealt with boots before. He sniffs them and 'manifests disgust', just as he did yesterday. Given just a trace of memory, the intellect very quickly forces its world into familiar, deadening patterns of habit. Only a completely new experience can jolt it into productive new devices. Such experiences are deeply disturbing, and as we shall see, Vladimir will move as quickly as he can to push this one too into familiar pigeonholes.

The thief in the song

In the meantime, he consoles himself with a round-song, celebrating repetition. The pivot of the song is death. It does not, however, say simply, as Lucky did, that dying is a fundamental part of living. Instead, it describes death as something humans are responsible for. The controllers of the world and its resources (the cook) and all their underdogs ('all the dogs' who 'came running') join forces to dispose of anyone who disturbs the way things are, however small his challenge and however great his need (stealing 'a crust of bread'). The cook kills the thief and the other dogs bury him deep and use him as a cautionary tale to bind future generations. What is striking is that Vladimir sings the tale to himself, cautioning himself against rebellion. He is closing more tightly the doors of his own prison-house.

So far, he and Estragon have cheated the tomb just as in the song, repeating the run-up over and over again, without change. Vladimir assumes that sticking to the same routine is what has saved them from the darkness. But he is not sure, and as he sings, he constantly stumbles over the 'tomb'. Presumably his fear is that one day – as his song does – they will find themselves despite all their efforts permanently stopped. The opening of this act is different from the first in that it makes clear the imminent threat of an ending that hangs over the whole of existence. Under the overt threat of death, the action of Act 2 will be more intense and faster-moving.

Estragon enters and the routine is repeated of the rejected embrace and the enquiry into Estragon's beating. There is also an echo of Vladimir's earlier suggestion they should repent. Vladimir explains how he would have defended Estragon, had he been there, by stopping him from doing whatever 'they' were beating him for. He will not accept Estragon's insistence he was doing nothing. In Vladimir's anxious world, every event has to have a cause and every punishment must have a crime. In its absence he will invent one, trapping and deforming reality in the net of his 'reason': 'The truth is there are things escape you that don't escape me, you must feel it yourself' (p.60).

There is unintentional irony here. Nothing *is* in fact real for Estragon unless he has literally felt it, which puts him several steps closer than Vladimir to reality. Yet Vladimir forces on his friend his own distorted versions of truth. He presses Estragon to say he feels happy they are together again: 'Say you are, even if it's not true' (p.60). There seems little point in Estragon doing this, since Vladimir himself has just admitted he has no idea what 'happy' means: 'Perhaps it's not the right word' (p.59). As he becomes more wedded to his routines, his anxiety intensifies, and his logic, increasingly, goes to pot.

Remembering

However, whatever the true nature of their state, one thing remains settled; they're waiting for Godot. Vladimir embarks, as before, on his attempts to convince Estragon this is the place they were to meet Godot, where they waited yesterday. Estragon can't remember the tree, nor Pozzo and Lucky. He dimly recalls 'a lunatic who kicked the shins off me. Then he played the fool' and someone else who 'gave me a bone' (p.61). Since he only remembers what he 'feels', it is interesting to see the range of things that impress him: pain, the satisfaction of hunger, and diversion (in its double sense of 'entertainment' and 'distraction').

Vladimir's insistence on remembering and recognising infuriates Estragon. This sudden movement from calm to frenzy is a regular pattern in the play, which brings out again humanity's eternal oscillation between passivity and action. Estragon denounces Vladimir's obsession with 'scenery' and 'landscapes' (and behind that, his delusion that Godot's place is any better than this one). His next insult ('You and your landscapes! Tell me about the worms!' (p.61)) unwittingly hits on a crucial point. It is much more useful to know about the worms, those underground forces who can transform a landscape. To put it another way, if the couple tried, just for once, to look below the surface, and recognised all the repressions and suppressions that have shaped their world and themselves, they might get somewhere more interesting.

Vladimir has to be given points for perseverance. Out of the blue, he brings in the Macon country and tries to make Estragon remember a

visit there. Estragon has no memory of it at all and nor, it turns out,
has Vladimir, who can't remember whose fields they picked grapes
in, nor the name of the place.

Playing dead

Estragon suggests again they part, and then offers a new way of doing
this: 'The best thing would be to kill me, like the other' (p.62). To a
disconcerted Vladimir ('What other?'), his only answer is: 'Like
billions of others'. Like Christ, he perhaps means, especially in view
of his remark at the end of Act 1 that he has always identified with
Christ. The implication would be that Vladimir and his kind always
destroy those who, like Christ, want a new life. Vladimir's answer is
the complacent cliché, 'To every man his little cross', which is
frightening in its unrecognised implications. Vladimir would seem to
be saying: those who want change are sent to try us, but we can put
up with them and see them off.

Playing talk

At Estragon's suggestion, they try to converse calmly. Their first
effort is a low-key, lyrical little conversation, as empty as the rustling
of the leaves in the wind, whose sound it echoes (pp.62–3). The
emphasis at the start of this exchange on the word 'like' ('like
wings' . . . 'Like leaves' . . . 'Like sand' . . . 'Like leaves') raises for
the audience an important point about language and the impossibility
of using it to express reality simply and directly. A vague approxima-
tion, 'like', is the most truthful statement that can be managed.

The dead voices they don't want to hear are like leaves, according
to Estragon, but he doesn't say what kind, alive or dead. Vladimir
suggests both. They are like wings and feathers (open, free images)
and like sand and ashes (images of sterility and death). The past to
which the couple are tied sounds alive but is really finished. The
language of the past that they speak seems to offer words with which
they can free themselves, invent dreams of escape. But the dreams,
like the words, are really hollow and dead.

A conversation on that kind of theme makes a lovely poem but it
gets nowhere. It simply sticks in the dead leaves. A second attempt
(pp.63–5), examining the basic patterns and machinery of conversation ('That's the idea, let's contradict each other'; 'That's the idea,
let's ask each other questions') does better. This too comes to a
dead-end, though not so fast, in three mind-twisting ambiguities: 'To
have thought': 'We could have done without it'; 'Que voulez-
vous?'.

The first two are Vladimir's, the end of a train of thought stretched over the whole dialogue. 'Thinking is not the worst . . . What is terrible is to *have* thought'. Does he mean it is worse to possess thought, or to have finished with thinking? 'It's not the worst, I know . . . But we could have done without it'. Does he simply mean he would rather not have thought, or is he going a step further and saying that thinking prevents doing? '*Que voulez-vous?*' is Estragon's phrase. 'Ah well', a sigh of resignation, is its idiomatic meaning. More literally, it can mean 'What do you want?' This little comment homes in on the central problem of the play. If they knew what they really wanted, they wouldn't be messing about here; they would possess the answer to the question of the meaning of life, the gold at the rainbow's end, the mystery lurking in the Holy Grail, the real meaning of Godot. They will never know what they want, for all they have to look for it with is thought and language, in all their inherited corruption. So Estragon's last ambiguity is crucial. As Vladimir echoes, with unconscious irony: 'Ah! *que voulez-vous*. Exactly'. 'What you want' isn't exact at all.

Doing nothing

Reassured by all his familiar routines, Vladimir is able now to confront the problem of the leaves on the tree. According to Estragon, they are evidence that this is not yesterday's place. Vladimir seems to concede this (p.66). Having conceded the point, like a true intellectual, he ignores it, and concentrates instead, as usual, on *making* it yesterday's place, bullying Estragon into remembering Pozzo and Lucky and making him concede that the boots on the ground are those he discarded the day before. In this sequence, Estragon resembles Lucky, addressed as 'pig' and pushed and pulled about, the weaker person used by his stronger partner to make the partner feel more secure. If the pain of the Pozzo–Lucky relationship is here turned to comedy, this is basically because Estragon puts up more resistance: 'All that's a lot of bloody – ' (p.67). But Vladimir holds two trump cards, like Pozzo: the rope that keeps Estragon with him ('We're waiting for Godot') and the promise of food. The second is as empty as Pozzo's promises: no carrots left, or pink radishes, only a mouldy black radish and turnips. The conclusion of this sequence is not merely ambiguous but proliferates possible meanings:

VLADIMIR: This is becoming really insignificant.
ESTRAGON: Not enough. (p.68)

Is Estragon sulking, grumbling he isn't getting enough? Or threatening Vladimir, by implying that 'This' must become much more insignificant, that Vladimir must stop stuffing their world with invented meaning – especially if all he can come up with in the end is a black radish. Estragon knows when he is being conned: 'I only like the pink ones!'

And yet he is easily won back by the diversion of putting on his boots, and re-enters the game with eager gullibility:

ESTRAGON: We always find something, eh Didi, to give us the impression we exist?
VLADIMIR: [impatiently]. Yes yes, we're magicians. (p. 69)

Estragon's eagerness to believe Vladimir is no different from the eagerness of the faithful to believe the one Gospel-writer who says one thief was saved. It springs from the same source ('It's the only version they know', Vladimir had explained) and it is very tempting to apply to Estragon his own comment at the time: 'People are bloody ignorant apes' (p.13).

The unexpected discovery of Lucky's hat, which Vladimir adopts as his own, is a timely reassurance that this is the right place, and inspires a game of Pozzo and Lucky. Estragon, to his credit, proves incapable of playing Pozzo, even with prompts. Vladimir ends up playing both parts – the intellectual doing his bit to make sure the pattern of exploitation goes on.

And indeed, it would seem that opting out of the exploitation game leaves Estragon with no place to go. Having rushed off stage, he rushes back on in panic, to shock Vladimir out of his game. 'They' are everywhere, and there is no place to hide. In the last resort, the two stand 'Back to back like in the good old days' (p.74). Out of this episode, they manage another conversation, made up of ceremonious politenesses, insults and words of reconciliation. Exercises follow, finishing with the yoga balancing position 'the tree'. A joke reference to God (whose watchful eye upholding all creation would not seem to be having much success with the wobbly yogi) suddenly turns sour. Tired of the game, Estragon screams out, 'brandishing his fists': 'God have pity on me!' (p.77). What starts as just play ends in violence and pain.

Second Block: Pozzo and Lucky

God, or whatever disposes the universe, answers with the return of Pozzo and Lucky. Pozzo is now blind and so the rope that ties Lucky to him is shorter. The weaker the master, the tighter his rein. Startled by the unexpected confrontation, he and Lucky bump together and collapse helpless among their baggage.

Again, Estragon mistakes the new arrival for Godot. Vladimir does not, but is still delighted. These are 'reinforcements' to help them 'to see the evening out', a diversion which causes him to lose all interest in Godot: 'Now it's over. It's already tomorrow' (p.77). In the French, Estragon is more conscious that this relief is only temporary: 'But they're only passing through'.

Inevitably, the man of business and the intellectual, joined in such an unnatural way, trip each other up and fall in a helpless heap. Vladimir and Estragon suddenly find themselves in control of the situation, but with no sense at all of the chance it offers to make some very significant changes. They have several choices: to help Pozzo and Lucky up, to help them up at a price, or to leave them there. What might make most sense is to rescue Lucky and deal separately with the problem of Pozzo. But they can't do that, partly because they are so used to thinking of them as inseparable, and partly because they have swallowed Pozzo's story that Lucky is the one to fear: 'For the moment he is inert. But he might run amuck any minute' (p79).

Vladimir squares up to the situation with a rhetorical detachment worthy of Pozzo, speaking of mercy and humane responsibility instead of practising what he preaches. At last he moves to help. Whether he is impelled by his own humanitarian sentiment or by Pozzo's offer of two hundred francs is not clear. Perhaps it is money and sentiment together that drive him to reinstate the fallen tyrant. Not unexpectedly, instead of pulling Pozzo up, he finds himself pulled down in the heap beside him. At least once down he has some clearer notion what kind of people he is with, calling to Estragon: 'Don't leave me! They'll kill me!' (p.81).

Estragon is not seduced by Pozzo's cash. He is repelled, in fact, by Pozzo's stink. What draws him to help is partly Vladimir's promise that they will go away for ever, somewhere really nice, together, but most of all his own affection for his friend: 'Come on, get up, you'll catch a chill' (p.82). He too is pulled down into the heap.

This is a pantomime situation, and hysterically funny, but it is also very serious. Dragged down with the master and his slave, Vladimir and Estragon find that they still have the upper hand. They are used to coping with being at the bottom of the heap, whereas Pozzo needs help. But a change of position is not a change of nature, and they throw another chance away. When Pozzo asks 'Who are you?' (p.82), Vladimir is still a proud rhetorician ('We are men') and Estragon doesn't know who he is but is lost in blissful communion with 'Sweet mother earth!' They can only seek to 'pass the time' (p.83) at the bottom of the heap, just as they did at the top. Finally, when they try, they find themselves back on their feet. But, unable to leave because 'We're waiting for Godot', there is nothing left to do except help up Pozzo. The Godot trap now leaves them, literally, with Pozzo round their necks. Estragon's resentment is justified, but the problem is self-inflicted: 'How much longer must we cart him round? We are not caryatids!' (p.86). The answer would seem to be they are stuck with him now, until he decides himself to get off their backs.

Despite his blindness, Pozzo still exerts a strange authority over the tramps. The questions he asks (who they are, what time it is) imply he is dependent on them but at the same time they force a certain kind of answer, in the same way as Vladimir's questions to the Boy determined the Boy's replies. Vladimir, who calls Pozzo 'sir', still looks to him for confirmation that his own obsession with time, place and the past (being determined to wait for Godot) is a sensible one. He joins Pozzo in urging Estragon to revive Pozzo's 'menial' (p.87), Lucky, with a few kicks. With a rough comic justice, Estragon merely hurts his own foot, while Vladimir's expectations of fresh entertainment and encouragement from Pozzo are cruelly disappointed: 'Don't count on me to enlighten you' (p.88).

Lucky meekly hands over the whip and rope to Pozzo. He is dumb, so useless now to anyone but Pozzo. The old world of money and authority and the culture that ratified it must stand or fall together. His menial restored, Pozzo's self-confidence is assured, despite his blindness: 'Certainly I am Pozzo' (p.88). Holding on to Lucky, Pozzo regains his old control over words, impressing his own blind man's despair on the sighted Vladimir. For the Pozzos of the world, all days are the same and life is short and cruel, almost indistinguishable from death: 'They give birth astride of a grave, the light gleams an instant, then it's night once more' (p.89).

Even when he has gone, his influence on Vladimir lingers: 'I wonder is he really blind . . . It seemed to me he saw us' (p.90). Estragon, who was fast asleep, locked in his own bad dreams, while Vladimir was undergoing his nightmare of disillusionment is categorical: 'You dreamt it' (p.90). His reply is truer than he knows. Pozzo's authoritarian reality and Vladimir's dream of a Godot who will take over all his responsibilities are indeed the same thing. In fact, pressed by Estragon a moment later, Vladimir is no longer completely sure that it wasn't Godot who just passed. The trap has closed tight. Even Estragon has now fully entered Vladimir's dream, answering his own 'Let's go' with the 'We can't' that used to be Vladimir's line.

Third block: the Boy

There is none of the conversation between Vladimir and Estragon
that opened this sequence in Act 1. Estragon has fallen asleep again
and Vladimir is reduced to monologue. He wonders how much of the
suffering and sleeping is indeed his own dream, no more than his own
desires imposed on reality. He briefly runs over the basic elements of
his life's dream-drama, rehearsing a tomorrow which will be just like
today and yesterday: waiting with Estragon for Godot, speaking to
Pozzo and Lucky as they pass, Estragon waking and remembering
nothing, describing his beating, and eating a carrot. Then he runs
over that life again in the language of despair Pozzo has just given
him, but in an even shorter, more cruel version. In Vladimir's
experience, the grave reaches out in anticipation for the unborn baby
('the grave-digger puts on the forceps') and life is a long, screaming
decay into old age. And he asks: 'In all that what truth will there
be?'

He is on the same treadmill as Lucky, his drama getting shorter and
swifter as it reaches the end. This little speech is a kind of embedded
Act 3. It is formally and tightly enclosed inside the two-act structure,
but points outside to an interminable stretch of repeats in the tramps'
own future time, out of our sight. In a few brilliantly brief words it
also points to a stretch of interminable repeats in another direction,
or even dimension. Perhaps the Vladimir watching Estragon dream is
also a dreamer watched by someone else (p.91). This is of course the
case; we, the audience, are the watchers. There are any number of
possible alternative perspectives on the situation Vladimir and Estragon are caught in – any number of alternative 'truths' about it. With
the benefit of the critical perspective which a second day's experience
has given him, Vladimir has glimpsed something that could be vitally
liberating. There is no absolute reality, only an infinite number of
perceptions and interpretations of it, all made in the light of our own
prejudices, desires and dreams. There are no fixed points of knowing
anywhere, and never any waking up to absolute truth. His reaction is
not relief, but fear: 'I can't go on!'

Vladimir concludes his monologue: 'What have I said?' This
expresses, perhaps, his horror at its implications. Perhaps it also
implies that he has forgotten what he said, and so the frightening
insight it gave rise to can also be forgotten. But forgetting, like
remembering, is not so easy. What he now knows and represses
changes Vladimir's next dialogue with the Boy.

The Boy enters. This time there is no indication he is afraid. Again
he addresses Mr Albert, and Vladimir again wearily accepts the new

name. The interview has a different tone. Vladimir no longer asks eager rhetorical questions but makes flat, hopeless statements, with which the Boy always agrees. It is almost as though Vladimir is seeing confirmed his suspicions that all this is his own dream. When he seeks new information, all he gets are empty answers. The Boy met no-one on the way, Mr Godot does nothing, the Boy doesn't know if he or his brother came the day before. One question only is answered, vaguely. Mr Godot has a beard, a white one, the Boy thinks. Vladimir's response – 'Christ have mercy on us!' (p.92) – could be exasperation at the Boy's vagueness, panic at Godot's likeness to the judgemental Jehovah of tradition, or horror at discovering age and decay even in the dream refuge. The proliferation of possibilities is deliberate, and the dramatic effect is to inspire in us Vladimir's own despair at the immensities opening up before him. He stops asking questions.

The Boy takes the initiative out of his hands and demands that Vladimir make a choice. What is he to tell Godot? Vladimir could confirm the appointment or tell Godot to forget it. Instead, he dodges the responsibility and hands the decision on his future back to Godot, giving away his rights yet again: 'Tell him . . . that you saw me'. The Boy slips away from his pouncing hands, the image, perhaps, of a future that can never be seized before its own ripe time. The tramps' mistake is to try to catch that future prematurely, by weaving their Godot-trap.

The drama winds down inevitably to its close. Estragon wakes up, puts his boots centre stage and joins the motionless Vladimir. 'Let's go' is no longer relevant. They *must* go and start again, now the moon has risen and the day is over. 'Where shall we go?' is the question, and he has the right idea: 'far away from here' (p.92). Vladimir still resists; they've to wait for Godot. Estragon, with his refreshing, if naïve, disrespect for power suggests they drop him. But Vladimir is trapped by his own bogeyman: 'He'd punish us' (p.93).

In the despairing silence, one symbol of hope and change remains. Vladimir notices it: 'Everything's dead but the tree'. This is the tree of which he earlier complained it was no use for hiding or hanging and so no use at all (p.74). It is still of no use to them, because they are blind to the message it carries of natural renewal. Preoccupied with their own survival in the immediate present, they are incapable of placing themselves in larger, more liberating perspectives. So they go on asking the tree the hopeless, petty questions which are the only ones they can think of asking: What kind is it, and can they hang themselves on it?

Vladimir says hanging is out. They must wait once again for Godot. The ironic circle is closed. If they weren't, metaphorically, hanging around waiting for Godot, they wouldn't be suffering so. But waiting for Godot is all that stops them, literally, from hanging. What they want is a better vision of what they want. They must let go of their present vision – Godot – to find it. But they daren't let go, out of fear of the unknown which is what they really want. They end up eternally wavering and quavering in the conditional ('*unless* Godot comes', '*if* he comes'), still busy with their poor, wobbly imitation of 'the tree', hoping God is watching them, when the real thing is staring them in the face.

The concluding image pulls together all the grotesque, pathetic and heroic qualities of their blind perseverance in folly. They reaffirm their commitment to each other. They'll hang or be saved together. They put themselves in order for the next day. Vladimir puts on Lucky's thinking cap, which he's made his own, and straightens up the disorganised Estragon as best he can ('Pull on your trousers'). Never mind the grief of the body; think of the civilized conventions. They conclude in balance: words of going, coupled with no movement, neither end nor beginning, an equilibrium which is very nearly stasis. Their closing words are exactly those of the close of Act 1. The only, minimal, difference is that the speakers exchange lines.

3 THEMES AND ISSUES

3.1 THE COLLAPSE OF WESTERN CULTURE

The philosopher Theodor Adorno, characterising *Endgame*, spoke of the unfolding of 'an historical moment . . . Since the Second World War, everything, even culture, apparently reviving, is in fact in ruins, without knowing it: humanity vegetates, going on crawling after events that even the survivors cannot survive, on a heap of ruins'. Adorno's perception applies equally well to the rest of Beckett's fictions. What Beckett offers, through his various characters and landscapes, is a vision of the collapse and decay of Western culture and society.

This vision has its immediate historical origins, but it belongs also within a tradition. Beckett's work and perceptions fall clearly within the ambit of the Theatre of the Absurd. Absurd drama was first launched on a horrified Parisian public in 1898 with the first brief stage appearance of Alfred Jarry's *King Ubu*, an obscenely comic caricature of the bourgeois violence, rapacity and bad faith which in Jarry's view were tearing apart the moral fabric of his world. It was preserved and developed in the thirties by Antonin Artaud, creator of the Theatre of Cruelty and co-founder of the Théâtre Alfred Jarry, and proliferated from the fifties and sixties through the work of Beckett, Ionesco and Boris Vian, the latter a cult figure of 1968 student revolt. All these writers take as their subject the hollowness, decadence and fundamental absurdity of the Western world. Their drama pierces through the tissue of lies on which Western man has built his heroic self-image and presents in its place the end of the civilized illusion, the end of civilization and the end of the hero. It is the language of this culture that has created and perpetuated its lies; and the aim of absurd drama is to tear language apart, until it discloses its deceptions.

3.2 THE ABSURDITY OF THE WORLD

Waiting for Godot is a dramatic re-enactment of the unrecognised absurdity of the world that is lived and perceived by Beckett's contemporaries. The drama is absurd in two senses. In the first place, it is ridiculously funny, as is most of Beckett's writing. Placed in the perspective of eternity, in the shadow of death that the living can never forget ("Where are all these corpses from?' (p.64)), the antics with which the characters fill their short span are ludicrous. All are levelled down to the same laughable status: Estragon's laments over his aching feet, Vladimir's complaints of his friend's sweaty socks, games of losing, finding, swapping hats and boots, suicide attempts, debates on damnation.

That particular translation of 'absurd' as comic is Beckett's dramatic version of its other, philosophical sense. His black, obscene, pantomime humour is an attempt to bring life-preserving detachment into a situation so atrocious that to view it head-on could only produce a formless cry of depair. An absurd world is a frightening one. It has in itself no norms, no absolutes, no consoling certainties, no direction. It simply exists. Nothing and nobody living in it has any pre-ordained sense or purpose. These same assumptions underlie the existentialism of Albert Camus and Jean-Paul Sartre (key figures of the Parisian intellectual scene from the forties onwards) which eventually re-shaped the post-war imagination, running parallel with the dramatists' vision.

To say that life is absurd is to challenge head-on the two great acts of faith on which Western culture is founded: reason and religion. Confidence in reason is the basis of belief in human ability to order and control the material world. Religion, especially Christianity and its personal God whose Providence directs history, gives an over-arching assurance that everything is in control. These are the two languages with which Vladimir and Estragon must make sense of their world, and they would seem to be just so many empty words. In Beckett's own words, there is nothing but words, divorced from all meaning: 'It all boils down to a question of words' (*The Unnamable*, p.308).

3.3 THE TRAP OF RELIGION

The Christian tradition is the particular tragedy of the characters in *Godot*. Their imaginations are filled with half-remembered images, stories and models of behaviour from the Bible: the Dead Sea, pale

blue ('I used to say, that's where we'll go for our honeymoon' (p.12));
the two thieves; John the Baptist, Christ's precursor ('I'm leaving
my boots there. Another will come, just as . . . as . . . as me, but
with smaller feet, and they'll make him happy' (p.52)); the crucified
Christ himself ('All my life I've compared myself to him' (p.52)).
Godot is not God, but a symbol who performs for Vladimir and
Estragon the same kind of dream Father-function. They are conditioned to expect a revelation and an ending to be given them,
'someone' to come and distribute, arbitrarily, rewards and punish-
ments and, they hope, provide a final refuge. They expect to be given
meaning. The truth is that the only meaning in existence is what they
construct themselves with their own words and acts. As Lucky says in
his speech: 'for reasons unknown no matter what matter the facts are
there' (p.44).

An existentialist vision of life, which says all meaning is in the
present, not in the past or the future, represents a radical change of
perspective. It was not one a fifties audience, only recently intro-
duced to such concepts, could easily accept, which explains much of
the hostility with which the play was originally received. For a
post-sixties audience, it should be less of a difficulty. For the
characters in the play, it is an unanswerable challenge, not least
because most of the time they have no idea that there is a problem.
Sometimes they have a glimpse of the dead-end they are in:

VLADIMIR: We're waiting for Godot . . .
ESTRAGON: We came too soon.
VLADIMIR: It's always at nightfall.
ESTRAGON: But night doesn't fall.
VLADIMIR: It'll fall all of a sudden, like yesterday.
ESTRAGON: Then it'll be night.
VLADIMIR: And we can go.
ESTRAGON: Then it'll be day again. [Pause. Despairing.]
               What'll we do, what'll we do! (p.71)

But they try to repress their unease, with decreasing success and
increasing anguish.

They double their own misery. There is always the pain and
struggle of the fact that life is only what you make it. By trying to avoid
that struggle, and make someone else responsible for their existence,
they only put off the evil moment when they must face facts for
themselves. And they add the fear and uncertainty of what their
invented 'protector' might do to them. The image Beckett uses to bring
this metaphysical anguish down to earth is Vladimir's bladder

trouble. It hurts him to pee, but as Estragon says, it hurts much more when he insists on waiting to the last minute, trying to put off the inevitable. As Vladimir ruefully confesses: 'Hope deferred maketh the something sick' (p.10)

For those who are blind to the absurdity of the world, life is a nightmare of self-inflicted pain. Completely disorientated, though claiming to know where they are, they can have no confidence in their own definitions of reality. They can't tell whether they are asleep or awake. Vladimir asks himself: 'Was I sleeping, while the others suffered? Am I sleeping now? Tomorrow, when I wake, or think I do, what shall I say of today?' (p.90).

They are caught on a treadmill of their own making, dooming themselves to repeat forever the same tedious cycle. Critics have seen similarities between their waiting state and the sufferings of the souls in Dante's Purgatory, which Beckett much admired. But though some of the torments may be similar, there is a basic difference. Purgatory is a place of atonement for sins which the sinner repents and which someone will finally forgive. In Beckett's materialist world, no-one will forgive because no-one has sinned. Estragon categorically rejects Vladimir's suggestion that they repent: 'Repented what? . . . Our being born?' (p.11).

The treadmill they have made themselves is also a trap. They have given away their freedom by tying themselves to Godot; they've 'got rid of their rights', as Vladimir says (p.19). Sleep offers no escape, for the unconscious world of dreams only re-enacts in more frightening forms the repressions and the terrors of the waking life. Death is no solution. They only 'play' hanging to bring some excitement into their tedium:

VLADIMIR: It'd give us an erection.
ESTRAGON: [highly excited]. An erection!
VLADIMIR: With all that follows. Where it falls mandrakes grow. That's why they shriek when you pull them up. (p.17)

They try to leave one another, but they can't. They try to leave the plateau but at its edges are the mysterious 'they' who administer unprovoked beatings and the 'bog' which is the audience.

The place where they are caught is full of fear. They are frightened of everything unknown, frightened of the silence, frightened of the Godot of their own invention, frightened of other men. They have no reason to fear the unknown and the silence. They have every reason to fear Godot and the other authority figures they have invented in his image, having conceded them all power to punish. It is no accident that the first man to cross their path is the arch-intimidator Pozzo. Displacing shapeless fears into real forms makes very little sense. The silence doesn't go away, and now there is more besides: cruelty, violence, humiliation.

3.4 THE TRAP OF REASON

The language of reason weaves similar traps. Vladimir applies the absurd instruments he has learned to call 'intellect' to justify the equally absurd act of faith by which he defines their space as the place of waiting for Godot. Forced to start afresh every day to chip sense out of his world, his first concern is always to 'prove' that this is the same place he was in yesterday. There might be considerable advantage in assuming a relatively fresh beginning is being made; which is, indeed, the case, as all things are in constant change. But Vladimir feels safer when he is using habit as a screen between himself and his fears: 'The air is full of our cries. But habit is a great deadener' (p.91).

In his essay on Proust, Beckett denounced the power of habit to destroy life:

Habit is a compromise effected between the individual and his environment . . . the guarantee of a dull inviolability, the lightning conductor of his existence. Habit is the ballast that chains the dog to his vomit. (pp.18–19)

Though in the short-term it might make living easier ('Breathing is a habit'), its long-term effects are deadly.

Vladimir depends on two faculties to restore the sense of habit to his day's activities: reason and memory. Neither, it seems, as the day runs down, are to be trusted. Vladimir is increasingly frustrated by his failure to fix firm defining points in time or space – Estragon's boots, the tree, the memory of time spent in the Macon country. For Beckett, in a world always in flux there is nothing to be known but change. Individuals are in a state of constant change, like every element in the world about them, so change is all they can ever know: 'The observer infects the observed with his own mobility' (*Proust*, p.17). Neither Vladimir nor Estragon will recognise this. They discuss Pozzo and Lucky:

VLADIMIR: How they've changed! . . . Haven't they?
ESTRAGON: What?

VLADIMIR: Changed.
ESTRAGON: Very likely. They all change. Only we can't. (p.48)

'Reasoning' is a frustrating exercise. Objects yield no hard information, only vague, slippery words. Estragon's boots could be black
or brown, or else a kind of grey, or perhaps rather a kind of green.
Estragon has the right description: 'All that's a lot of bloody –'
(p.68). Reason itself is suspect. Even Vladimir begins to question it at
the end of the second day. Their ploys for filling in the time seem
reasonable to begin with, but not so when they become habits,
mechanically repeated. They do these things to stay sane. But
perhaps they've never *been* sane. Perhaps the whole world is mad.
And the final irony of this mad world is that it can't be questioned
except by using the language of reason. 'You follow my reasoning?',
he asks Estragon (p.80), who is not much comfort: 'We are all born
mad. Some remain so.' This is Alice's confrontation with the
absurdity of Wonderland and the assurances of the Cheshire Cat:
'I'm mad, you're mad, we're all mad. You must be or you wouldn't
have come here'. And Beckett and the cat seem to have found the
same way to cope: brief, acute, not unfriendly comment and then
departure, leaving on the air an enigmatic, lingering grin.

3.5 MEMORY AND TIME

Memory has gone the same way. Where, when and even why the two
are supposed to be waiting for Godot is very vague: 'What exactly did
we ask him for? . . . I can't have been listening' (p.18). Memory
depends on a sense of time. But in an absurd universe, time doesn't
exist: it is only one more human, subjective way of trying to impose
meaning on the meaningless.
  Each of the characters has his own particular way of relating to
time. Pozzo, the professional man, clings to his watch. If he wants to
conduct his business efficiently, he must affirm that he controls and
regulates time – other people's, as well as his own:

VLADIMIR: Time has stopped.
POZZO: [cuddling his watch to his ear]. Don't you believe it, sir,
          don't you believe it. Whatever you like, but not that.
          (p.36)

His description of the natural beauty of twilight is punctuated by
references to the time on his watch. Losing his watch is a major

catastrophe. The great tragedy of his blindness is that it leaves him completely dependent on others for the time of day.

Vladimir's equivalent of the watch is his own memories, which he tries to convince himself and Estragon are correct. Estragon must accept Vladimir's 'yesterday' for Vladimir to be able to set today in his habitual patterns. Beckett wrote in his essay on *Proust*: 'There is no escape from yesterday because yesterday has deformed us, or been deformed by us . . . Yesterday is . . . irremediably part of us, with us, heavy and dangerous' (p.13). In one sense, of course, this is true. The past shapes the present. But how absolutely and inevitably it does so we don't know. Beckett struggles to break free; Proust and Vladimir voluntarily chain themselves to their culture's past versions of itself. So many of the memories Vladimir tries to urge on Estragon are linked with death: the time Estragon tried to drown himself in the Rhone (p.53) or yesterday's tree that they almost hanged themselves from.

Estragon has no interest in remembering: 'I'm not a historian' (p.65). This is a healthy attitude, given that little that goes on in their lives is worth remembering. He has forgotten the visit to the Macon country because 'I didn't notice anything' (p.62). Vladimir's irate insistence – 'But down there everything is red! – proves the point. If everything is the same, nothing is worth bothering with. For the same reason, Estragon cannot 'recognize' today's place as yesterday's:

> Recognize! What is there to recognize? All my lousy life I've crawled about in the mud! And you talk to me about scenery! [Looking wildly about him.] Look at this muckheap! I've never stirred from it! (p.61)

Estragon's memory plucks a kind of subjective value out of the absurdity. 'Either I forget immediately or I never forget' (p.61). Forgetting is of two different kinds. Sometimes it is the most important, often painful, events of the past that are repressed and buried, usually with neurotic consequences. More often it is the trivial things that go, which did not matter at the time and are not worth remembering. Vladimir remembers the trivia in order to evade the crucial memories (Godot failing to turn up, Pozzo's inhumane treatment of Lucky). Estragon remembers what matters: keen physical sensations of pleasure and pain, the satisfaction of real needs, and other satisfactions associated with these. He may have forgotten trying to drown himself in the Rhone, but he remembers the bliss of returning to life in the hot sun.

It is only Vladimir who forces Estragon into the miseries of time, despite his weary resistance: 'Don't torment me, Didi' (p.66). Estragon begins his day relatively content. He remains untroubled when he casually concedes a past to please Vladimir: 'Yes, now I remember, yesterday evening we spent blathering on about nothing in particular. That's been going on now for half a century' (p.66). But with this concession, he is trapped. By the time Vladimir has finished spinning his precise recollections, Estragon may say he has had enough, he wants to leave, but it is too late. Vladimir is now determined, and Estragon with him: 'We're waiting for Godot' (p.68). Vladimir's memories drive Estragon to grief and despair. Beckett quotes Proust's own comment on such situations: 'If there were no such thing as Habit, Life would of necessity appear delicious to all those whom death would threaten at every moment, that is to say, to all Mankind' (p.29)

But as Beckett's own play shows, Proust is only half-right. There is here one more ludicrous paradox. Without the habits of Vladimir, who destroys his happiness, Estragon could not survive. Feckless, lacking time sense, able only to react, never to take initiatives or forethought, Estragon would be lost without the friend who gives him carrots and radishes, helps him on with his boots, finds him something to do. Vladimir's confidence is not entirely convincing: 'When I think of it . . . all these years . . . but for me . . . where would you be . . . ? [Decisively.] You'd be nothing more than a little heap of bones at the present minute, no doubt about it' (p.9). But he has enough of a point not to need to worry about Estragon's threat they should part: 'You always say that, and you always come crawling back'–(pg.62).

The life lived by absurd creatures in an absurd world is riddled with all the contradictions and paradoxes Beckett found in his *Proust*:

Time – a condition of resurrection become an instrument of death; Habit – an infliction in so far as it opposes the dangerous exaltation of the one and a blessing in so far as it palliates the cruelty of the other; Memory – a clinical laboratory stocked with poison and remedy, stimulant and sedative. (p.35)

4 TECHNICAL FEATURES

4.1 CHANGED CONVENTIONS

In the usual format of the Master Guide series, this section would be headed 'Plot and structure'. It should be clear from the preceding sections that it would be foolish to try to force Beckett's drama into such conventional categories, without a little preliminary thought. Beckett's drama aims to subvert conventional ways of organising, planning, and stifling the real matter of the world in which we live. It does not believe that the world can be analysed, psychoanalysed, sliced, wrapped up and packed away with the confidence that traditional writers show. Much of the pleasure or pain an audience derives from the play comes from having 'normal' expectations of the patterns of playwriting set aside and being asked to work out an entirely new way of seeing things – an immensely liberating or frustrating experience, depending on the spectator's prejudices. This is not to say there is no order in the play. It is, however, an order of a new kind, which is generated by the subject-matter and not imposed on it.

First, briefly, what has the play *not* got? There is no plot, in the sense of a narrative with beginning, middle, end: exposition, twists and turns of intrigue, crisis and unravelling. Vladimir and Estragon do their best to invent a plot, 'waiting for Godot', but it hardly gets off the ground. There is simply a situation: two men loitering with intent, under a tree. There is no structure, in the sense of a neat carving-up of the action into three or five acts, with scenes advancing in logical sequence, entrances and exits motivated and the whole wrapped up at the end and finished with a bow. There is a string of tableaux with gaps between them, that lurch into movement haphazardly, grind to a halt like rundown clockwork, and stop altogether when the light goes out. There is nothing in the stage set to give you an inkling of what the play is about. The dialogue is enigmatic and leads nowhere and none of the characters really seems to expect it to.

Yet once preconceptions are set aside, it becomes evident that there are very clear structuring principles at work in this play. The general way the drama moves has been characterised as a double pattern: chain and circle, or line and spiral, both movements operating simultaneously.

The chain image is more helpful than that of the line to describe how the tableaux are strung together in sequence, as the couple experience them. Activity starts from a minimal point, develops and proliferates, and then dwindles down again, to be followed by a pause and then a fresh beginning on a new link. Chance determines a start. Something crops up – an object, a person, or more rarely, an idea – that is a pretext for doing. Surprise and disorientation are built into the structure and experienced by characters and audience alike.

But overall, the tableaux can be seen to fall into roughly regular patterns. Each act contains the same three points: activity before Pozzo and Lucky arrive; activity with Pozzo and Lucky; activity after, including the coming of the Boy and the fall of night. For his Schiller Theater rehearsals, Beckett divided Act 1 into 6 scenes and Act 2 into 5. In each act, two scenes preceded the Pozzo–Lucky confrontation and one followed it. In Act 1, the Pozzo–Lucky scene contained three episodes and in Act 2 it contained two.

The circle image conveys the closed, endlessly repetitive nature of the kind of life these characters are caught in. A second act doubling the first is just enough to hint at an endless series of empty echoes, particularly when Vladimir himself picks up the notion at the end, in his monologue over the sleeping Estragon, and foresees tomorrow's rehearsal of the same old thing. This same monologue brings an extra even more terrifying dimension to our understanding of the play's structure, as Vladimir ponders on Estragon dreaming, re-enacting in his dreams the repressions, fears and failures of his waking life, and wonders if someone is watching him as he watches Estragon. There is not just the one simple circle of history being enacted on stage, but a whole series of circles, in many dimensions, countless closed and enclosing perspectives focused on the simple action Vladimir sees. Out of the structure emerges a very important fact. There are no fundamental realities to be pinned down. There is only layer on layer of multiple, changing perceptions, which can never be grasped in a single vision.

Things in the circle are not *quite* the same the second time around, and in fact the spiral is a better image. In the human perspective, things get a little worse each day. (This is so in Nature's perspective too, though the process moves more slowly. The tree's sprouting leaves in Act 2 might be counted an advance, but is no more than a short-term gain. This close-up version of time – the spring, summer, autumn, winter which is about as much natural change as humans can measure – should be set against Lucky's overview of the universe from pre-history to post-history, gradually running down and dying back into its constituent parts.) As Pozzo says, the second pipe never tastes as sweet. In Act 2, there is less of everything: carrots, fresh radishes, vision, speech, and time. As the actors come closer to the death that is the underlying fact of all life, everything seems to speed up. Here again the structure of the play itself presents an important concept: the time we know, like all the reality we know, is subjective. The nearer we are to the end, the faster it seems to slip through our fingers.

The structuring principle of the double runs all through the text. Sometimes there is straight duplication. Gesture or mime repeat or underline verbal statements. Events are duplicated. Everything has an echo. This technique has a critical function. An observer cannot make sense of something without something else to compare and contrast it with. Duplication gives a critical perspective and with it the chance to think and make judgements about the doubled material.

More often than not, the doubling produces contrasts, oppositions, and contradictory meanings. The drama as we watch falls into ambiguity, double meaning. Everything seems to come in pairs: positive and negative, body and spirit. The drama reproduces life as we have learned to see it, and we have learned from our teachers, theologians and philosophers to see double.

In his book on Proust, Beckett admired Proust's perception of the way all things seem, to the human observer, to fall into two contradictory parts. He thought it the great achievement of Proust that he managed, at occasional, privileged moments, to join the doubles together again through the magic of art, so that a hero who passes most of his life in a sense of anguish, anxiety and incompleteness in the end experiences the liberating relief of finally being whole: 'Thus at the end as in the body of his work, Proust respects the dual significance of every condition and circumstance of life' (*Proust*, p.69).

Feeling torn in two and longing to be whole is not a *necessary* part of being human. We experience it in our culture as a hangover, be it from rationalism, Romanticism, or Christianity. Beckett's drama makes no comment on the truth or otherwise of our symptoms. All he's interested in is making us aware of the *shape* they have come in. When critics say that the drama of the two thieves is the basis of this play, it is not because there is any hard information about salvation or damnation to be extracted from that episode. It is because that 'either-or' pattern is the only way we know how to give form to our struggles to find a meaning. Beckett has said:

> I am interested in the shape of ideas even if I do not believe in them. There is a wonderful sentence in Augustine. I wish I could remember the Latin. It is even finer in Latin than in English. 'Do not despair; one of the thieves was saved. Do not presume; one of the thieves was damned.' That sentence has a wonderful shape. It is the shape that matters. (Quoted in Harold Hobson, 'Samuel Beckett, Dramatist of the Year', *International Theatre Annual*, No 1., London, John Calder, 1956, pp.153–55)

Ruby Cohn has listed the incidence of doubling in *Godot* in her article in *Journal of Beckett Studies*. There are two acts, two days, and two similar sets of incidents within them. There are two couples. Each couple is a unity of opposites. One tends more to the intellect, one tends more to the body. (The clown character they all share is itself traditionally a double blend of the pathetic and the grotesque.) The doubling is given physical shape on stage. In Beckett's own Schiller Theater version, the link within each couple was expressed by costume. Vladimir and Estragon both wore hats and dinner-suits. In Act 1, Vladimir had a dark coat and striped trousers while Estragon had the reverse; in Act 2, vice versa. Lucky's trousers and Pozzo's jacket were both grey; Lucky's jacket and Pozzo's trousers were brown check. (The Boy wore a plain light shirt and trousers, presumably to indicate that he was still a relatively blank sheet.) Tall thin Vladimir contrasted with short plump Estragon, but both walked in step, fell in the same way, and rose simultaneously. Even the object-couple, tree and stone, mirrored the same pattern, tall and squat, organic and inorganic. Cohn points out: 'The doublet is Beckett's main scenic rhythm'.

She adds though that triplets are also an important part of the structure. (Any lyrical or rhetorical statement, aiming to persuade, from a love song to a speech by a politician or a general, will give evidence of how basic to language exchanges the triplet pattern is.) There are three degrees of light in each act (twilight, darker twilight after Pozzo and Lucky leave, and moonlight after the Boy goes).

When Beckett directed Lucky's speech, he specified three speeds (slow, speedup, frenzy) for its three-part statement (God, Man, Nature). Between them, these double and triple rhythms carve shape into the otherwise formless anguish of waiting for Godot.

One final point. Audiences, well-primed by critics, are now able to understand that *Godot* is a very carefully structured play. The original watchers, confronted with unfamiliar patterns, were forced to struggle to make sense of a language they hadn't yet learned and that struggle was itself part of the meaning of the play. There is a pleasant irony here, that afflicts all avant-garde theatre. Eventually, the techniques a dramatist uses to challenge his public's habits and conventions themselves become familiar and automatic, and lose their subversive force. As a reviewer commented when Roger Blin revived the play at the Théâtre de France in 1961:

> This is theatre marked out with a compass and built with a plumb-line . . . Eight years ago . . . this was not as perceptible. Construction was effaced by surprise. Surprise is dead, what remains is a somewhat too methodical arrangement. (Pierre Marcabru, *Arts-Spectacles*, 10–16 May 1961, cit. and tr. *The Critical Heritage*)

We might ask what is left when the pleasure of surprise is gone. I would answer that surprise and confusion are entertaining, but a good writer knows their effects are short-lived. Once surprise is replaced by familiarity, an audience is free to give its attention to something more difficult but far more shocking and interesting: that is, the *words* of the play. The longer the audience focuses on these, the more aware it becomes of the endless, disturbing, hilarious possibilities of meaning which, mercifully, no critic will ever have taped.

4.2 CHARACTERISATION

Shaped as they are by the same culture, the characters share a number of common features. Each is split by the same contradiction. On the one hand, he knows himself chiefly as a separate, isolated individual. At best, he is indifferent to other people's needs: Vladimir and Estragon consistently disregard each other's suffering, preoccupied with their own pain. At worst, he consciously refuses to part with anything of himself or his possessions. Pozzo declares himself owner of all the land about, conceding others may pass through on the road but it's 'a disgrace'. He hoards his food in his picnic basket, giving away only the bones. He isn't self-possessed, in fact, for he depends on Lucky for his place in the world; but he says he is, and that authoritative self-confidence gives him his power over others. The retreat into self is also a defence mechanism, a product of fear of others which to a large extent would seem to be justified by experience.

On the other hand, each is driven to form some kind of relationship with others, by need, greed, and sometimes by compassion. A solitary existence is a material impossibility. But relationships can be of very different kinds. Pozzo and Lucky, master and slave, are joined artificially and by force, with their rope, while the partnership of Vladimir and Estragon, though not a voluntary one, seems to be based on genuine mutual need and relative equality.

Even so, all the relationships between characters are to different degrees based on the exploitation and abuse that Beckett observed in a Europe occupied by Hitler and an Ireland occupied by Britain and the Churches. Vladimir and Estragon make use of each other to ward off the fear of loneliness or the unknown. But they also share each other's fears (huddling together cringeing at the sound of Pozzo's approaching cry, standing 'back to back like in the good old days' to protect their space against imagined terrors). Together they turn anxiety into something useful, making conversation to make the time pass. In the Pozzo–Lucky pair, there is no co-operation. Lucky is the paid entertainer who does all the work, while Pozzo takes all the credit.

Pozzo's attitude is infectious. Vladimir and Estragon quickly learn to despise Lucky and enjoy watching him forced to perform for them. Vladimir even wants to play-act their degrading relationship afterwards, though Estragon resists. The symptoms appear in them of the violence that exploitation thrives on and breeds. Pozzo's rope scars Lucky's neck; Lucky kicks Estragon; Estragon kicks Lucky, when he's down. As Estragon comments in Act 2, after the pair have gone, crucifying one's neighbour seems to be normal practice.

Poverty, scarcity and lack have left their mark on all the characters except the Pozzo of Act 1. And things are getting worse. In Act 2, even Pozzo is under threat. This in itself is a cause of their fear, selfishness and violence. Commodities – things – are a vanishing resource, to be envied and fought over. Food, the basic material of survival, is a doubtful quantity. In Act 1, Pozzo gets roast chicken, while the others are lucky to share the bones. Vladimir supplies Estragon from a scanty store of vegetables that shrinks in range and quality as the day goes on. The objects (pipe, whip, watch) that are the signs of Pozzo's wealth and status are mysteriously lost. The characters' own physical and mental faculties are in decay. Estragon has one sore foot in Act 1 and two in Act 2, not to mention the wound on his leg where Lucky kicked him. Lucky, practically worn out when he first appears, is even worse in Act 2 and dumb to boot, while Pozzo has gone blind. No one is very firm on his feet at any point and in Act 2 all end up collapsed in the same heap. Little confidence can be placed in memory and the powers of reason and even less in language, whose decay is, perhaps, most frightening of all.

The two principal figures, *Vladimir* and *Estragon* are not heroes of the drama by any classical definition. This is a play about the human condition, but it is not cast in the mode of high tragedy that convention would lead us to expect. Beckett calls it a 'tragi-comedy'. Its matter is the ordinary stuff of everyday life and its characters the common men of modern times. Getting by is their major preoccupation and salvation for them means simply food, sleep, shelter and some relief from pain and fear.

They are not tragic heroes but pathetic clowns. Like the tramps in whose guise they are often portrayed, they are shabby (or rather, shabby-genteel) survivors, permanently poised, squirming and teetering, on the edge of disaster. Yet in their own context they can seem heroic and even admirable, just like Chaplin or like Laurel and Hardy, those other clowns in modern dress. Given their limits, and the limits of the muck-heap which is their material and cultural inheritance, they do well to snatch the little they manage from the mess. Spiteful, selfish, opportunistic, they show nevertheless redeeming flashes of tenderness and compassion and their perseverance is impressive even if the cause to which it is devoted is absurd.

Roughly speaking, they present what Western philosophy, since René Descartes, the seventeenth-century founder of modern rationalism, has believed to be the two opposite but complementary sides of the individual human subject: matter and spirit, body and mind. The tall, thin Vladimir fits the stereotype of intellect, restlessly articulating, questioning, analysing, keen to pin labels, fit facts into categories, hasten to conclusions. When Estragon asks what kind of tree theirs is, his ignorance is first honest and then authoritarian; what he doesn't know he'll make up, rather than admit himself at a loss: 'I don't know. A willow.' Estragon, who declares himself closest to 'sweet mother earth', is more passive, slower, and drawn to silence and sleep rather than speech. Content to accept what is, he figures the version of the body we have learned from Descartes. (Beckett had studied Descartes' work closely, and also that of his Belgian disciple Arnold Geulincx.) Estragon is almost completely dependent on the activity of the mind for his nourishment and guidance. He takes his lead from Vladimir – not all of whose ideas, it should be clear, are good ones. The intellect is the major source of damage and despair. It is fortunate that the body puts up a resistance to it, and perseveres in the face of intellectual desperation.

From the audience's point of view, the two characters only exist as a pair. Apparently they are separate during the night, but why and how we don't know. Action that takes place off-stage, beyond the limits of our perception, is simply not a reality for us and we can't comment on it. Beckett deliberately points the mystery of the way body and mind relate, in order to make his audience aware of the limits of their knowledge. We have working hypotheses to explain how humans are constructed and how they behave, but we must recognise that these are only inherited guess-work.

There are other indications in the way the characters are constructed that the simple body-mind distinction, like so many of the simple fixed oppositions we have to work with, may not be a perfectly satisfactory concept. There is no way we can know anything definite about identity. The human matter we observe is in a constant state of flux, and we ourselves, the observers, are constantly changing and changing our position. And we look at our subject through a frame of assumptions and prejudices we can never be fully aware of. Human identity is not a matter of fixed relationships but of oscillating relationships between an unknowable 'self' and other points 'outside'. The image of this uncertainty is Pozzo, lying blind and fallen, answering equally to all names his ignorant interlocutors place on him: Cain and Abel, guilty and innocent, executioner and victim. As Estragon remarks: 'He's all humanity' (p.83).

Vladimir and Estragon are what Ruby Cohn has called 'symmetrical opposites', opposite and yet alike – a point made clearly in the costumes Beckett gave them in his 1975 Berlin production (see above, p.46). Between them, they share all the contradictions of human nature. When Lucky falls (p.22), the stage direction says *both* are half eager, half afraid to go to his help. Dramatically, this has to be simplified to be seen, so Vladimir moves forward and Estragon pulls him back, followed by the appropriate phrase for each. This does not necessarily mean that intellect is always altruistic and body is always selfish. The rough distinctions are there, but they are not absolute. A reader could cover up the names on the page and have some difficulty guessing who had said what. It is seeing the characters physically, on stage, with all their differences exaggerated, that makes them easier to tell apart. Estragon can be brusquer, and ruder – though interestingly, this shows less clearly in the English version, where some of his replies are sharper, wittier and more serious than the original French.

They have their own roles, but sometimes they swap them. Estragon is passive and sleepy. When Vladimir (p.69) looks for an 'occupation' or a 'recreation' to pass the time, Estragon prefers a 'relaxation'. When Vladimir suggests 'exercises', 'elevations', 'elongations', 'to warm us up', Estragon contributes 'movements', 'relaxations', and again 'relaxations', 'to calm us down' (p.76). He opens the play with the first 'Nothing to be done' (p.9), against which Vladimir, the man of reason, argues in favour of effort ('I resumed the struggle'). Yet it is Vladimir who at the end of the sequence twice reiterates 'Nothing to be done' (p.11). And Estragon whose suddenly insistent probing shatters Vladimir's calm confidence. Is that a tree, or a bush? Were they really in the same place yesterday? Vladimir grumbles: 'Nothing is certain when you're about' (p.14).

Estragon, as critics point out, has bad feet, and they oppose this *physical* weakness to Vladimir's *intellectual* uncertainty. But Vladimir has bladder trouble, equally physical. Both have bodies that stink. Some critics have triumphantly commented that Estragon stinks from his feet (physical) and Vladimir from his mouth (speech, therefore intellectual). As Vladimir indignantly points out, his breath smells because he eats garlic for his kidneys' sake (p.17) – his problems too, then, are really physical. Pozzo also stinks, from a place whose symbolism no one has yet analysed, sickening even Estragon ('Who farted? . . . It's revolting!' (p.81)). All humans stink, but the masters, it seems, stink more than most. All humans are rooted in a fundamentally material universe.

Estragon was once a poet, as should be obvious, he says, from his rags (p.12). He still has dreams in his sleep. Pushed to it by Vladimir's unexpected failure to give a lead, he can still create new, if unexciting, things to do:

ESTRAGON: Tell me what to do.
VLADIMIR: There's nothing to do.
ESTRAGON: You go and stand there. [He draws Vladimir to extreme right and places him with his back to the stage.] There, don't move, and watch out. (p.74)

In short, our whole notion of character is built on a very easy opposition (body and spirit) which is not completely true and can lead us into gross misperceptions. Thinking by opposites is too simple, and often wrong. It is Estragon who (intelligently) raises the point, as he chews on his carrot:

> ESTRAGON: Funny, the more you eat the worse it gets.
> VLADIMIR: With me it's just the opposite.
> ESTRAGON: In other words?
> VLADIMIR: I get used to the muck as I go along.
> ESTRAGON: [after prolonged reflection]: Is that the opposite? (p.21)

Seeing things as opposites is just a habit, which Estragon is right to challenge. If the characters, and the audience, could get used to putting their thoughts into something other than these simple boxes, something different might perhaps be said.

Pozzo, to the disappointment of the two friends, is not their Godot (p.22). It might be said he is Lucky's Godot, for he serves the same function for Lucky as Godot does for Vladimir and Estragon: he gives him something to do in return for his patronage. If Vladimir and Estragon could view their situation with the distance that we have, as audience, they might draw some useful lessons about the kind of patronage and protection a Godot will give.

Nor, as some critics have suggested, is Pozzo God, although he is happy to be treated as a divinity by lesser mortals:

> POZZO: You are human beings none the less. [He puts on his glasses]. As far as one can see. [He takes off his glasses.] Of the same species as myself. [He bursts into an enormous laugh.] Of the same species as Pozzo! Made in God's image! (p.23)

Pozzo is the type of the Victorian entrepreneur – some kind of professional man, he says (p.33) – but at the end, unfortunately, of the Empire he helped to build. In Pozzo, Beckett displays the operations of authority. He shows how power is won and kept, and he demonstrates the viciousness and violence of rulers.

Pozzo is powerful because he assumes power, because he 'acts powerful', and because he knows how to wheedle others into his drama, whether by force or flattery. He wants servants and an audience to ratify his every move, walking, standing or sitting, to make his figure into the 'natural' centre of the landscape. Pozzo knows, because Lucky has taught him, how to handle language, both gesture and speech, and how to turn it into a rhetoric, an instrument of persuasion. His magnificent entry with cracking whip, loud voice, baggage, slave violently jerked on the end of a rope, is calculated to intimidate. He declares himself the owner of the land, and nobody asks for proof. He puts Vladimir and Estragon in their place with his laughter, and his magnanimous concession that they may walk along the road. He has a watch, with which he can define his own time and the time of the day. He can even define the time of year: 'Touch of autumn in the air this evening' (p.24).

He owns all the basics for survival and more besides: rich food and drink, a coat, things to keep his things in, a servant, a whip to keep the servant in line, a footstool, spectacles and a throat spray to make up for his physical deficiencies, a pipe for drugged pleasure. He has far more than the others have and far more than he needs. 'The fresh air stimulates the jaded appetite', he remarks, as he takes out chicken and wine before their envious eyes. Yet he eats 'voraciously' (p.25), as though he can never have enough.

He needs nevertheless, as he admits, the company of others: 'I cannot go for long without the society of my likes' (p.24); 'I don't like talking in a vacuum' (p.30). He enjoys bending others to the service of his law and order. He is a tyrant, who likes his bag, stool, servant placed just so, who dictates when he can ('Closer! Back! Further! Stop!') and when he cannot, hides his dictation under the hypocritical language of politeness: 'With your permission', he says, already sitting down, 'I propose to dally with you a moment, before I venture any further' (p.24).

He sits callously indifferent as the tramps examine the sore on Lucky's neck. He is not actively cruel, except in revenge. He looks on people as commodities, objects for use; feelings don't enter into it. Tears and laughter are for him quantifiable items on a balance sheet: 'The tears of the world are a constant quantity. For each one who begins to weep, somewhere else another stops. The same is true of the laugh' (p.33). Contempt is his strongest emotion, though he can play-act pity or grief when it suits him. In this way he deflects Vladimir's attack on his callous treatment of Lucky, claiming melo-dramatically that he suffers far more than Lucky does, while Lucky stands silent, unable to plead his own cause. Immediately the point made, he drops the mask: 'Forget all I said. I don't remember exactly what it was, but you may be sure there wasn't a word of truth in it. Do I look like a man that can be made to suffer?' (p.34). The amazing and distressing thing is that this naked cynicism does him no harm. Vladimir and Estragon, the clear evidence of it before them, shut ears and eyes to the obnoxious side of Pozzo and accept the image that he dictates. This is partly because their own longing for distraction will induce them to accept anything, even a holocaust, as long as it's someone else's:

> ESTRAGON: It's awful.
> VLADIMIR: Worse than the pantomime.
> ESTRAGON: The circus . . . He's a scream.

It is also because Pozzo knows how to play on their weak spots. The way to make them stay with him is to remind them that this is the place where they have their appointment with Godot. Pozzo has no reason to believe in the appointment, nor even in Godot, but it suits his purpose to act as though he does.

There are hints in Act 1 that Pozzo is less powerful than he claims, as he loses pipe, whip, throat spray and watch in succession. It is clear he has nothing of value to give in return for his listeners' time and attention, except Lucky's garbled rhetoric. He can't function without their applause (p.38) or Lucky's assistance. He can't even leave the stage without Lucky to pull him. In this, as Estragon observes, he's just like any other mortal:

> POZZO: I don't seem able . . . [long hesitation] . . . to depart
> ESTRAGON: Such is life. (p.47)

Estragon is more sceptical about him than Vladimir. Yet both eventually accept him at his own valuation:

> VLADIMIR: That passed the time.
> ESTRAGON: It would have passed in any case.
> VLADIMIR: Yes, but not so rapidly.

In Act 2, Pozzo is almost unrecognizable, blind and vulnerable to the point where Vladimir, urged by Estragon, can cheerfully kick him. This point is not reached until all four are helpless on the ground and Pozzo's selfish screams become too irritating, even for this patient pair (p.84). Pozzo no longer rules time. Watch gone and sight gone, he has no instruments to shape the world: 'The blind have no notion of time. The things of time are hidden from them too' (p.86). He is dependent on others, much more obviously than before, and Estragon, for one, sees little advantage in wasting his time propping this crumbling façade: 'We are not caryatids' (p.86). Yet, instinctively devious and cunning, he still dominates. He still knows others' weaknesses and how to play on them. He still promises rewards he will never have to cash. He will never admit to being vulnerable. Pressed by Vladimir to admit he is Pozzo, the wreck of the glorious creature they met the day before, he refuses to remember. Memory of defeat is inconvenient. Where before he boasted of his memory, describing the twilight the others must have seen before, but had forgotten, he now implies with consummate bluster that memory is of no importance:

> I don't remember having met anyone yesterday. But tomorrow I won't remember having met anyone today. So don't count on me to enlighten you.

He can still make Vladimir feel small, and make him believe everything he says. Just as in Act 1 his version of nightfall was accepted unquestioningly, now his equally unsubstantiated (and highly pessimistic) version of life is swallowed without demur: life, he says, is no more than a flicker of light between birth and the grave. Vladimir is intimidated: 'He told us he was blind. . . It seemed to me he saw us' (p.90). Fallen father-figures still retain their power to impress their dark vision of their own failure on those who will listen and believe, despite the evidence, in their own weakness and the master's strength.

Lucky, bottom of the pecking order in this drama, must take much of the blame for making the muck-heap on which they all now live. White-haired, shaky-legged, sick, confused of speech in Act 1 and dumb in Act 2, his role is to support Pozzo and all that belongs to him. He will never change. Pozzo may threaten to sell his slave, but the slave will still not rebel. He will listen to no-one but Pozzo – and Pozzo takes care this remains so. When the others try to speak to Lucky, horrified by his condition, Pozzo interrupts with sham concern and a command of his own: 'Leave him in peace? Can't you see he wants to rest? Basket' (p.26). When Vladimir and Estragon pose a simple, sympathetic question – 'Why doesn't he put down his bags?' (p.29) – he lets Pozzo answer for him, which Pozzo rapidly does, eager to present his own version of their unequal relationship. Any possible sympathy that might develop between his three subordinates is skilfully nipped in the bud by Pozzo, and it's not surprising that Lucky's first direct communication with what he seems to regard as a new and inferior brand of tormentor takes the form of a violent kick in Estragon's shins. Lucky could have judged the others by their acts. He might have noted Vladimir's passionate defence of him against Pozzo, as well as Estragon's intercepting his bones (a nice manoeuvre there on Pozzo's part). But he doesn't, blind and deaf to his real interests, just as Vladimir and Estragon are.

Lucky is apparently responsible for arming Pozzo with the language of morality that covers up his selfish lack of morals, and with all those rhetorical skills that enable the unscrupulous to manipulate the vulnerable. Pozzo makes no secret of it:

> Guess who taught me all these beautiful things. My Lucky! . . . But for him, all my thoughts, all my feelings, would have been of common things. Professional worries! Beauty, grace, truth of the first water, I knew they were all beyond me. So I took a knook. (p.33)

Lucky is the intellectual, the man of ideas and words who has sold his skills to conserve, instead of criticise, a corrupt society. He is not a philosopher but an entertainer, a song-and-dance man, and not a very good one any more. Concepts that are conserved without criticism fall into stagnation and decay, and Pozzo has every reason to cringe at the flood of rubbish the worn-out machine pumps out. (From another perspective, it could be argued that Lucky's tirade brilliantly fulfils the intellectual's duty, which is to hold up to society a mirror of itself. But it must be added that Lucky is certainly not performing this function consciously. The wreck set before us is incapable of such deliberate mockery. A Beckett can hold up such a mirror, but not an old, sold-out entertainer.)

Lucky's fate shocks Vladimir and Estragon, though they learn nothing from it. There is a deep irony in the drama. Vladimir, the intellectual and would-be authority, tries to model himself on the self-assured Pozzo. What he actually finds himself imitating, in the game of 'playing Pozzo and Lucky' which Estragon sensibly refuses to take part in, is *both* of them. In the end, he is just Lucky. He picks up the intellectual's hat from the floor and keeps it. The stage business he performed with his own hat at the beginning is repeated at the end with Lucky's hat: he peers inside, shakes it to get out what's stuck there, and puts it on. With it, he puts on all the corruption of Pozzo's world. It is not only Pozzo's physical violence and bullying that sustains the master's power. It is also the more insidious force of the intellectual tradition, which urges, as Lucky did in his speech, that authority, scientific reason and death are the natural, fundamental principles of the universe. Death is certainly so; authority and scientific reason are equally certainly not, and only Lucky's persuasion ever made anyone think they were. At the end of the day, it is Lucky's own fault that Pozzo can dispose of him so easily, because Lucky has recruited so many to Pozzo's service: 'As though I were short of slaves!' (p.31).

The Boy is well-nigh impossible to characterise, since he does not have even the beginnings of a defined character. He is the unknown of the future, hovering in the wings, nervous and timid. He is almost entirely at the mercy of his elders. As far as he can, he gives the answers their questions require. Whether or not those answers are true always remains to be seen. He has little new information to give, and what he can give is hardly worth knowing. The Boy shows that questioning the future provides little reassurance and much ground for fresh unease – far better to get on with the present.

He cannot be pinned down by violence, though both Estragon and Vladimir try. He comes at the appointed time, obeying some constraint fixed on him from outside, but not their constraint. He gives them no more than a modicum of reassurance and just enough hope to make them go on. The future is not going to be determined by people who will not move off the muck-heap.

The Boy calls for a Mister Albert, and Vladimir accepts the name. Vladimir cannot pin down the future, but the future can determine him. This seems only fair. Vladimir is cheating the present of its rights by dreaming up a mythical future, waiting for Godot when he could be doing. In return, the future strips him of his rights (or rather, as he said, he gave them away). It takes away his name and guarantees him no place.

In one sense, the Boy carries a pessimistic message. For Vladimir and Estragon, he is the future made in their own image: Godot's Messenger, a vague dream of impossible salvation. But their despair, it must be remembered, is subjective, as was Pozzo's. The Boy is also the bearer of a kind of optimism in the drama. His simple appearance is a reminder that there *is* a future. It is not necessarily the future the couple see; indeed, the Boy's words to them are cryptic and evasive, and he wriggles away. But it exists, and will be one more story out of which something different might possibly come. The Boy already belongs to Godot, and the corrupting conversations of the old world have begun to weave their net round him too. But he is still a fresh pair of eyes, and a pair of fast-moving feet, and he starts from a different place.

Beckett's *presentation* of his characters requires a last general comment. Like the drama as a whole, they are not realistic in the conventional nineteenth-century sense of the term. Beckett does not want to create an 'illusion of reality' through which his audience can identify themselves with his characters. That kind of identification often makes a play popular because it fit its version to the idea of reality the audience has been trained to have. Instead of telling the audience the truth about itself, it tells it what it wants to hear. Characters that are 'nicely rounded', 'convincing', 'analysed in psychological depth', their origins explained and their behaviour coherent even if unpleasant, encourage the assumption that we are coherent subjects in a coherent world. An audience would rather identify with what it would call 'villains' than what it would call 'lunatics'.

Beckett's characters are presented with the very special realism of absurdist theatre, and can usefully be compared with the creations of Alfred Jarry, Eugène Ionesco, or Harold Pinter. Their presentation aims to make the audience do a double-take. Many of the things they say or do strike a spark of recognition. We use the same gestures and phrases and the same clichés. But the way *they* use them does not quite make the sense we think *our* phrases make. As a result, instead of identifying with the characters we distance ourselves from them. With the detachment that follows, we can begin to recognise a fresh set of truths about human behaviour which have a quite different and compelling 'reality'.

Beckett's characters act in a way that reveals that they, like us, are fundamentally stereotypes. In a sense, they are prefabricated creatures, whose every act confirms and reinforces that prefabrication. They are invented by styles, languages and forces outside themselves.

The language of the play, which will be looked at in the next section, is one of the means by which this effect is created. Beckett's use of the clown tradition is also very important. The clown offers a highly stylised version of human nature. He expresses his emotion in the depersonalised form of the jester's mask. His vices and virtues are grotesquely distorted, and his every gesture is exaggerated towards the ridiculous or the pathetic, or both. Martin Esslin commented on this in his review of Beckett's German production of the play when it appeared at the Royal Court in April 1976. Whereas other producers brought out the 'allegorical gloom and tragic pathos' of the play, Beckett himself, said Esslin, stressed the comic perspective, bringing out 'his deep indebtedness to popular entertainment, above all the silent cinema, the circus and the music hall'.

Esslin admired the skill with which each actor in this production placed his character into a different part of the comic tradition. Vladimir and Estragon followed Laurel and Hardy, or Abbott and Costello; Lucky's white face recalled the great clown Grock; Pozzo was one of the bully boys from the Keystone Kops. Esslin explained the implications:

It is a world of broad slapstick comedy: each character has his highly stylized mode of movement, circumscribed by the convention he has created for his own comic personality – and I, for one, find this a brilliant image for the concept of existential choice facing all of us.

The emphasis on recognisable styles underlines the fact that being a person is a question of falling into learned patterns. The beauty of the clown, all make-up and baggy costume, is that he displays this fact all the time. Literally, he wears his heart (sewn) on his sleeve. What Beckett's play shows is that all character is hand-me-down costume; personality begins at the point where the masker begins to be aware of his mask.

4.3 LANGUAGE

In this world of absurdity, where meaning either vanishes or proliferates beyond understanding, language itself plays a double role. It is the only instrument with which the characters can hope to know or control the world outside them but it can offer no true knowledge at all. Whatever they say about the world makes no difference. Reality remains outside the grasp of the language they have learned. And yet they go on speaking, for words are all they have. Estragon knows that to 'say', subjectively, that a thing is so will not make it so. But Vladimir perseveres, compulsively pinning down things with labels, as though an adjective ('that') were a cage:

ESTRAGON: In my opinion we were here.
VLADIMIR: You recognize the place?
ESTRAGON: I didn't say that.
VLADIMIR: Well?
ESTRAGON: That makes no difference.
VLADIMIR: All the same . . . that tree . . . that bog. (p.15)

Vladimir knows the answers he wrings out of Godot's Boy are empty of meaning: 'Words, words'. Yet after a pause, he adds: 'Speak' (p.50). This is the paradox on which all Beckett's work is built. Language is a poor, faulty instrument but there is nothing else to work with. Beckett's genius is to turn words against themselves, making them show up their own emptiness. His characters' misery comes from taking words at their face value. Vladimir and Estragon are reluctant to admit that the words are not so much their key to freedom as the stones of which their prison house is made.

As the drama runs its second round, in Act 2, the critical intellect is increasingly aware of the lie, the confidence trick, that is language. So as Estragon bustles towards a new diversion, delighted to have found something else 'to give us the impression we exist', Vladimir's comment is ironic: 'Yes, we're magicians' (p.69). The language the pair have inherited is a vehicle of illusion. It is a collection of techniques not for telling truth but for inventing and deceiving. When the conjurers are only second-rate, or when the gap between lie and reality becomes too wide, language has to own up to its trickery: and this is what this drama sets out to make it do. If the characters could see through language, they could also see through all those power structures it props up. They, of course, don't; but the audience, sitting at a distance, has a better chance.

Vladimir and Estragon rely on language to see them through their daily life. Time and again, it comes to pieces in their hands. They try hard to use language as they should, with the precision and clarity which the academic tradition teaches are the first steps in controlling any subject matter. It isn't pure desire for knowledge that drives them, but need. Vladimir feels he needs certainty. He labels a tree a tree, not a bush or a shrub (and as an extra flourish names it a willow) because he needs to convince his partner and himself that their anonymous space is the particular place of the appointment with Godot. Estragon needs to eat, and he distinguishes between a carrot and a turnip and a pink radish or a black one because not all, for him, are edible. Unlike Vladimir, he feels no need for extra flourishes. Vladimir's solicitous 'How's the carrot?' gets a laconic answer: 'It's a carrot' (p.20). Language that really works will satisfy authentic need and then fall silent. Vladimir has to go on spinning words because his need he's hoping to satisfy – Godot's coming – is only make-believe. It can never be satisfied, so he can never shut up.

The mere fact that your language is precise is no guarantee it represents anything real. The word 'carrot' lingers on long after the carrots are gone. Estragon's precise imitation of Pozzo devouring his roast chicken does not mean each is experiencing the same material satisfaction. As it happens, the mime in this case works almost like magic, and Estragon gets the bones – but only because Pozzo has his own reasons for giving them. It would seem that Vladimir and Estragon stick with the kind of language they're used to because in the short-term it still gives them enough to get by on. In the long term these short-term expedients produce more harm than good, like Estragon's insistence on cramming his feet into boots the audience knows are his old tight ones, despite his denials, or Vladimir's putting off peeing because of his bladder trouble, or Vladimir's inventing a future coming to calm his present fears. Like the language they speak (full of words like 'sir', 'death' and 'waiting'), these are all palliatives, that only delay the agony. On the other hand, what better language they might use is impossible to say. No one in this play is interested in fresh inventions, only in making do.

In the absence of anything else, trying to be precise is better than nothing. It fills in the silence, passes the time and stops things sliding together into grey, undifferentiated chaos. Estragon puts it graphically: 'Everything oozes . . . It's never the same pus from one second to the next' (p.60). Words can't fix meaning totally, but they can at least be used to make some slight discriminations out of the ooze, so the tramps go on practising: 'Our exercises . . . movements . . . elevations . . . relaxations . . . elongations' (p.76). They are not as good at making discriminations when it really matters. Admittedly, they are not confused by the closeness of the two names Godot and Pozzo into mistaking their wished-for saviour. They have every reason not to be: this terrifying figure is not the saviour they want. But they don't watch out for the smaller, subtler word-traps. Vladimir, hurrying to help up Pozzo, never notices a significant word-slip: 'A diversion comes along and what do we do? We let it go to waste. Come, let's get to work!' (p.81). Yet to know whether this action is work or play ('diversion') is crucial, if they are to understand what they're doing with their time. They think they're engaged in free play, but actually they're working for Pozzo.

While the characters are only dimly aware of the dangers of language, the audience sees their plight with painful clarity. Much of the dramatic pleasure - and unease - that the play produces is in the feeling of the language-ground shifting underfoot, sudden, estranging gulfs opening in the words and phrases that are the small change of everyday life. Mrs Rooney draws attention to the same problem in Beckett's radio play, *All that Fall*:

Do you find anything . . . bizarre about my way of speaking? [Pause.] I do not mean the voice. [Pause.] No, I mean the words. [Pause. More to herself.] I use none but the simplest words, I hope, and yet I sometimes find my way of speaking very . . . bizarre.

The language that can impose such effects on an audience must be a very special one. It sounds, at first hearing, 'realistic', just like our own spoken exchanges. If it were, we would be like the tramps, unable to get any critical handle on it. Instead, it is a stylised version of colloquial speech, reconstructed to set its hearers at the distance required for a critical understanding.

Real colloquial speech has quite different patterns from Beckett's play language. It is often incoherent, hesitating, jerky and most of all, crammed with redundancies. We communicate – struggling to get and hold our hearer's attention – by saying what we want to say over and over again, repeating ourselves, at unnecessary length, sometimes with over-emphasis, or else under-emphasis, and what we're trying to say in words, well, we back it up with masses of gestures, face, whole body, waving our hands – you know what I mean. The language of Beckett's characters is pruned down to the minimum and backed up only where necessary by equally pruned-down and stylised mime. Simple phrases stand stark naked in all their triteness. Pauses and silences are rarely hesitations. As in poetry, they are carefully placed at sense points, to create more coherence, not less. Colloquial jerkiness is smoothed out into lyrical or dramatic rhythms by judicious placing of commas, or subtle repetitions and balances, or the addition or subtraction of 'and'. For example, the sentence 'I would have stopped you from doing whatever it was you were doing' (p.59) could have been more roughly expressed as 'I'd have stopped you doing whatever it was'; the lengthier version is better balanced and more symmetrical. Or again, on the same page, 'I said to myself, he's all alone, he thinks I'm gone for ever, and he sings' would lose the dramatic swing to a climax if the second comma were replaced by the 'and' which in colloquial speech would be far more likely.

More obvious instruments of stylisation are the echoes and repetitions within the extended dialogues, such as the exercise variations referred to above. (Constant repetition always makes a word seem strange, pulling it loose from its usual context.) Or the deliberate juxtaposition of different styles in the same speech and even the same sentence, graphically demonstrating how uneasily this second- or third-hand, tacked-together cloak of language hangs on present-day shoulders. Pozzo's unintentionally comic account of twilight mixes the prosaic and the lyrical, the learned and the vulgar, elaborate rhetoric and simple onomatopeia, building to the climax when night bursts on us too, 'pop! like that!' Swapping insults on Vladimir's instructions ('Curse me!'), Estragon flounders gamely from one stylistic exteme to the next, 'Naughty!' to 'Gonococcus! Spirochaete!' (p.73). Tricks of rhetoric embellish the most ludicrously inappropriate situations. Vladimir and Estragon mourn softly and sympathetically over the fit of Estragon's boots, building up to the plangent 'Perhaps you'll have socks some day' (p.69). Estragon's

lyrical musing by the struggling heap of the fallen is rudely inter-
rupted: 'I've always wanted to wander in the Pyrenees. – Who
farted?' (p.81).

But the comic finds on the rubbish-dump of language can have a
cutting edge. Rhetoric can be dangerous. Vladimir's speech (see the
Commentary, Chapter 6) on the nobility of humane action holds up
the action it urges. In Lucky's speech, the display of the rotting
fragments of cultural style turns everyone's stomach and drives them
to murderous rage.

What self-consciousness the characters have about their language
develops in Act 2, where the initial focus is on the art and the use of
conversation. Two different kinds of conversation are set against
each other.

The first is a demonstration of the emptiness of language, used not
to probe a real problem but simply to fill the silence with elegantly
structured sounds. Vladimir and Estragon are trying to talk 'calmly',
to turn the panic of living and dying into manageable words, to ward
off the fear of the silent, unspeakable unknown: 'It's so we won't
think . . . It's so we won't hear' (p.62). Concealing the truth is the
traditional function of our inherited language. So when they speak
this way, what they summon up are 'dead voices', dry and sterile as
sand and ashes, not communicating, only rustling like leaves in the
wind. Such conversation brings more fear, not less, insinuating the
return of the insatiable dead ('To be dead is not enough for them').
Possessed by that past that lives on through language, the conversation goes nowhere, turning round and round on itself, and has only
one possible outcome:

ESTRAGON: What do we do now?
VLADIMIR: Wait for Godot.

When they try again, immediately, they do better. 'That wasn't such
a bad little canter', Estragon says complacently at the end. This time
they don't plan to be calm. They have no fixed aim. They simply want
to start, and so the future of their conversation is wide open: 'You
can start from anything'. This time they light not on the 'dead voices'
but a more active notion of searching: 'When you seek you hear'. No
doubt what you hear are still the 'dead voices' of corrupt language
and corrupt experience, but this time they brush that obstacle aside.
Instead of circling on the old, dead, known terrain, they move
forward, establishing the conditions of conversing: 'Let's contradict

each other . . . Let's ask each other questions', to which in a later exchange (p.75) they add interruptions and insults.

Vladimir brings the subject matter back to the unavoidable topic of the traces of death that corrupt all life ('A charnel house! A charnel house!'), but this time Estragon manages politely to deflect him: 'You don't have to look'. Clearly, to look on language as *process*, something to move forward with, a personal, even generous exchange with other people, and to try and establish how it works, even if it works badly, is a more fruitful way of handling it than simply to fix a fearful gaze on the traces of the 'dead voices'.

Before concluding this section, something must be said about the silence which is an integral part of Beckett's language and which has a meaning, or rather a range of meanings, of its own: 'It is all very fine to keep silence, but one has also to consider the kind of silence one keeps' (*The Unnamable*). Claus Zilliacus (*Beckett and Broadcasting*, 1976) has reminded us that silence has been part of theatrical language from the turn of the century. In the music hall, the technique of the comic pause has pointed comic failure to under- stand, or marked a punch line. In the legitimate theatre, with writers such as Chekhov, silence has been a means of increasing tension, illustrating incomprehension, inability or unwillingness to communi- cate, structuring monologues so as to intensify the loneliness of the speaker, and so on. Beckett uses silence in all these conventional ways. He illustrates, for example, the breakdown of speech with the mime Vladimir uses to get across his question about Lucky and his bags (p.31), or the frightened silence when the tramps confront the enigma of their relationship to Godot (p.19), or in Vladimir's final lonely, despairing monologue over the sleeping Estragon (p.90).

But Beckett also offers a reinterpretation of the entire nature of silence. It is an image for the different state of being that everyone desires, a new kind of language, if you prefer, so different that there are no words to describe it and no ways that we know to attain it. This is the state for which the image of being with Godot is a very poor substitute. Death is also the wrong image for it, though it is close (being also desired and feared, because wholly unknowable). Death is not what we want, because death is an ending of material existence, not a transformed way of living. Estragon's one attempt to evoke the nearest he ever got to happiness, and the one moment he truly remembers, is linked with death and silence. It was a suicide attempt, by drowning, from which Vladimir saved him. The near-dying is only memorable because it enabled him to feel afresh the pleasure of living. Similarly, the silence he falls into when he remembers doesn't indicate an absence of meaning, but rather a thrilling crowd of ideas, emotions, sensations beyond the reach of words. In the brief exchange that summons the recollection, everything that matters is 'said' silently, between the lines – Estragon's despair, astonished gratitude, tenderness, and the healing, material warmth of the sun on his newly-restored body:

ESTRAGON: Do you remember the day I threw myself in the Rhone?
VLADIMIR: We were grape-harvesting.
ESTRAGON: You fished me out.
VLADIMIR: That's all dead and buried.
ESTRAGON: My clothes dried in the sun.

Words can only be used to build the way to the threshold of the unknown, where they stop short. Beckett expects that 'The experience of my reader shall be between the phrases, in the silence, communicated by the intervals, not the terms, of the statement' (*Dream of Fair to Middling Women*).

Silence in Beckett's writing also expresses the sheer unknowableness of everything that is not ourselves, and our lack of power to pierce through to that unknown. It plays a vital part in presenting his understanding of the material nature of our experience. Unless the object –the voice outside – addresses us, we know nothing. We think the world is waiting for our minds to make sense of it. It is not. We have nothing except what the material world gives us; we are receivers, not generators, of sense. In the 1964 Royal Court production, which Beckett supervised, the actors were instructed to freeze and stare ahead at the end of their dialogues. The audience is at the mercy of the actors for everything it knows; the actors, in their turn, are at the mercy of the author who gives or witholds their lines. The audience can, of course, guess what the silence might mean, just as it guesses what the characters, or the play might mean, but the chances are that the reading that comes out reflects the prejudices that go in. Learning to discover and respect the limits of understanding is an important part of the experience of watching any Beckett play.

All knowledge is bounded by silence. Life is much less coherent and continous than we admit. Estragon, pressed by Vladimir to remember yesterday's self, denies that he can, and insists that there is no continuity and no communication between yesterday and today:

VLADIMIR: And where were we yesterday evening according to you?

ESTRAGON: How do I know? In another compartment. There's no lack of void.

4.4 STAGECRAFT

For the *setting*, the stage direction is simple: 'A country road. A tree. Evening. Estragon, sitting on a low mound.' This is the place where Vladimir and Estragon find themselves, relatively familiar and relatively safe. The road itself is not marked on stage, but its presence is clear from the other characters' passing and Pozzo's comment that it is free to all. The implication of the setting is that this place is very open.

Compared with some of Beckett's later settings, it certainly seems so. *Endgame* is played out in a bare-walled room with two high windows, with two characters legless in dustbins, and a third in a wheelchair. In *Happy Days*, Winnie sits buried up to her waist and then up to her neck in a disabling heap of sand. In *Play*, the actors are in funeral urns, costumed to seem made of the same earthy material as their containers. But as the action in *Godot* evolves, the characters turn the space into their own trap. The French version calls it a plateau, edged by a precipice. The English simply says: 'There's no way out' (p.74). There is the auditorium, but Estragon 'recoils in horror', presumably at the sight of a roomful of people just like him. Off-stage lurks the threat of a mysterious 'they' ready to beat up anyone reckless enough to try to leave. Others seem to be free to enter and leave the space at will. Vladimir and Estragon feel they are not.

Since the point must be that they make their own trap, a discreet director refrains from tightening the noose. This must be space with as little as possible laid down in advance, just the tree and the mound and in Act 2, the boots of Estragon's own placing. The tree needs careful handling. It is of indeterminate species. It is Vladimir who decrees it a willow, with all the lyrical associations of death and weeping that that implies. Alan Simpson, the play's first Dublin producer, thought it should be a skimpy tree, clearly an impossible vehicle for a hanging (*Beckett and Behan and a Theatre in Dublin*). This makes a sharp point: suicide is the couple's own choice, made only because it's obviously an impossible one, just for kicks. Vladimir and Estragon may believe that the shadow of death hangs over all, but they are not going to move into that shadow further than they can help. For the first Paris production, Roger Blin did a good job on the tree with a flimsy edifice of cardboard and coathangers. This had the added advantage of fitting easily into suitcases for the subsequent international tour. His Odéon production of 1961 was graced with a fragile tree by Giacometti.

The setting must evoke a universe that offers very little to work with, pre-empting many options but still allowing much of what happens to seem the characters' own choice. Simpson recalls Blin's original set at the Théâtre de Babylone, dictated by lack of cash, which has remained Beckett's favourite: 'some pieces of light green cloth (suspiciously like old double sheets) hung around the back and sides of the stage. This gave an exceptionally dreary effect, but in my view it looked amateurish' (p.131). Simpson preferred the solution found for his own Theatre Workshop presentation: 'a backcloth painted in browns and very dark greys, with a vague impression of roughly horizontal lines and a few little white dots . . . We found a small real tree, as in Dublin, and the bank or mound on which Estragon sits was small and angular . . . the ultimate result was completely negative and dreary, while at the same time professional and neat' (p.132). Peter Hall's Criterion set was beyond the pale, according to Simpson, 'too elaborate and interesting', with a cyclorama for backdrop, a large, practical stage tree far too suitable for a hanging, and assorted debris scattered round the stage, resembling a rubbish dump.

The *lighting*, like the tree, helps the characters make sense of their space. The fact that these characters only exist between twilight and nightfall is a fundamental part of what they are. They come in at the end of the day, when the work has already been done, and they have to make sense of the left-overs. Pozzo's speech focuses attention on the importance of the twilight time without explaining its real significance. (Being one of the masters, with a vested interest in shutting his eyes to the decay of his world, he doesn't know it.) All he can tell his audience is that in his country night comes sooner than you think – which is also truer than he knows. Cash problems at the Théâtre de Babylone produced not much light and a very creaky moonrise, which a well-disposed critic could have seen as underlining the man-made quality of a world all the characters take for 'nature'.

The kind of *stage* available for performances is a major factor in creating the right atmosphere between actors and audience. *Godot*'s initial success was closely linked with the availability of the little theatres, the Théâtre de Babylone for Blin's original production, or Simpson's Pike Theatre in Dublin, whose intimacy, as Simpson has said, could quickly create an atmosphere of hothouse excitement. Yet Simpson yearned to see the play set in a bigger theatre, to bring out what he considered the underlying magnificence of its vision:

In *Waiting for Godot* the objective of the producer should be to create the feeling that these four characters are isolated in Eternity . . . I think the ideal setting for this cosmic piece is a hugh stage where, in a little pool of light, Vladimir and Estragon, Pozzo and Lucky, perform their antics around the tree. The vast emptiness about their world serves to emphasise their dependence on one another and their isolation within the enormity of the universe. By the time the book is published, the play will have received such a production in Paris. (p.101)

Pierre Marcabru, reviewing that production (by Roger Blin, 1961), thought that the stage at the Théâtre de France was too wide and deep and that the tramps had not been properly directed how to 'occupy' it. As a result, he thought, the play had slackened and lost its impact.

Now that staging a Beckett play is enough of a paying proposition for a commercial director to have some choice of stage (in 1953, they took what they could get), the director has a greater responsibility for understanding just how much Beckett's tramps can cope with. As Ruby Cohn pointed out in the *Journal of Beckett Studies*, it must be they who are the focus of the action, operating in the empty stage space beloved by the great director and theoretician of Absurd theatre, Antonin Artaud, making 'valiant efforts' to move through it, bringing meaning into the emptiness, and gaining a 'movement-by-movement victory over stillness' with their 'stylised standing up, sitting down, walking about, and especially falling . . . (and) a half-dozen waiting tableaux'. This is what Beckett's own direction stressed in 1975 at the Schiller Theatre, instructing his actors precisely how to move and where to look. When there is too much space to move in, intensity is lost – unless Vladimir and Estragon are turned from little men into heroes larger than life, in which event the whole meaning of the play is transformed.

The characters' *costume* is very important. Though their behaviour is clownish, they should not dress as clowns. Beckett quietly discouraged Roger Blin from over-enthusiastic experiments in that direction and was disappointed to see it surface in the first Peter Hall production, on which he was not consulted. Though humans act like clowns, presenting grotesque stereotypes rather than authentic individuals, they are usually unaware of it. As Blin told Tom Bishop, for the *Cahiers de l'Herne*, 'The circus has to be perceptible, but as an undercurrent'. He added that all Beckett knew of the characters to begin with was that they had bowler hats. The deceptive dignity of ordinary modern clothes leaves it to the play of words and action to disclose the mask under the man.

Usually, Vladimir and Estragon appear as tramps in cast-off formal clothes. They are rundown versions of the conventional people who live at the centre of society, the same in kind, but tattered and living at the margins. It is the dwellers at the margins, simultaneously part of and rejected by their society, who have both the space and the motive to generate criticisms of it. These criticisms may sometimes be conscious ones, but more often they are not. A production by the Baxter Theatre Company at the Old Vic in February 1981 (reviewed in the *Journal of Beckett Studies*, No. 7, Spring 1982) emphasised the point by casting Vladimir and Estragon as blacks and Pozzo and Lucky as whites. The Boy was also black, which has interesting implications for the future. Alan Simpson's Dublin version gave the tramps Irish accents and cast Pozzo as a member of Anglo-Irish aristocracy, with Lucky in a gloriously decrepit footman's outfit which Simpson swears was a common fashion in Dublin families engaged in emulation of their English rulers.

This raises a general point of *interpretation*. Beckett prefers to have his plays staged as he wrote them, in a style which emphasises the crucial role of words and form in generating meaning. So presented, his plays are subversive and, indeed, political, but only in a very general sense. Attempts to harness his work to a particular system or philosophy are full of pitfalls. After all, that work says very clearly that all systems and philosophies are partial and self-interested views, generated by the same cramping language, and so always falsifications and simplifications of a reality that should be allowed to be as open as possible. Claus Zilliacus has written an interesting review in the *Journal of Beckett Studies* of one attempt to cash some of the political implications of *Waiting for Godot*. In his view, it didn't work, for the reason given above, but I note it here for the interesting light it casts on the relationship between Beckett's work and its contemporary theatrical, political and philosophical context.

The Lilla Teatern produced the play in Helsinki, Spring 1979, on a double bill with Brecht's *The Exception and the Rule*. Brecht's play holds the same privileged place in the theatre of commitment as Beckett's play does in the theatre of the Absurd. The contrast could not be more striking. Beckett's aim is simply to give an image of the absurdity of the human condition as experienced by his contemporaries. Brecht's priority, as a marxist, is not only to evoke that absurdity but to attack it as man-made and one that could and should be changed. The actors who played Vladimir and Estragon in the first half returned in the second half as Brecht's policeman couple.

Though Zilliacus thought this a falsification of Beckett's play, it seems to me that the point that is made is borne out in Act 2 by

Vladimir's eagerness to 'play at Pozzo and Lucky' (p.72). And on psychological and historical evidence, it is a sound one. When people are pushed out onto the margins of the society that has shaped them and then are forced by circumstances to take sides in that society's conflicts, their unreflective impulse will be to move to the side of the authorities responsible for their shaping. Those who do not see and understand the languages by which they are shaped can do nothing but join in and blindly further the process of repression. Estragon may try 'instinctively', for reasons he cannot give, to resist the cruelty of the game and opt out; but where does he go? Off-stage to the threatening unknown, to return in terror to the man of 'reason' ('He hastens towards Vladimir, falls into his arms') and blurt out the truth: 'I'm accursed!' (p.73).

Other technical questions I only have time to touch on here include that of the *balance* to be achieved between seriousness and farce and the question of *timing*, which is a major instrument of balance. Ruby Cohn has pointed out in *Just Play* the number of vaudeville gags Beckett delights in: 'unbuttoned flies, insistent bladder, dropped trousers, broken embraces, unexpected blows, speaking while chewing, juggling hats, manifest odors, and suicide feints' (p.11). George Devine, one of Beckett's English directors, has likened the problem of timing to that of harmony:

When working as a director on a Beckett play . . . one has to think of the text as something like a musical score, wherein the 'notes', the sights, the sounds, the pauses, have their own special inter-related rhythms and out of their composition comes the dramatic impact. (cit. A. Reid, 'From Beginning to Date: Some Thoughts on the Plays of Samuel Beckett', p.65)

Staging a text by Beckett is one of the great theatrical challenges. Determining the right actors, set, stage, pace, perspective and audience is fraught with difficulty. And even if each decision taken separately is a good one, the quality of the resulting cocktail is still vulnerable to the accidents of chance. Beckett's *Waiting for Godot* is a play that brings everyone involved in its making face to face with the material conditions of production. Staging it (just like watching it, or reading it) is dependent on the readiness of those involved to think through the whole process of how meaning is made.

5 SPECIMEN PASSAGE AND COMMENTARY: IDLE DISCOURSE

VLADIMIR: Let us not waste our time in idle discourse! [*Pause. Vehemently.*] Let us do something, while we have the chance! It is not every day that we are needed. Not indeed that we personally are needed. Others would meet the case equally well, if not better. To all mankind they were addressed, those cries for help still ringing in our ear! But at this place, at this moment of time, all mankind is us, whether we like it or not. Let us make the most of it, before it is too late! Let us represent worthily for once the foul brood to which a cruel fate consigned us! What do you say? [*Estragon says nothing.*] It is true that when with folded arms we weigh the pros and cons we are no less a credit to our species. The tiger bounds to the help of his congeners without the least reflection, or else he slinks away into the depths of the thickets. But that is not the question. What are we doing here, *that* is the question. And we are blessed in this, that we happen to know the answer. Yes, in this immense confusion one thing alone is clear. We are waiting for Godot to come—

ESTRAGON: Ah!

POZZO: Help!

VLADIMIR: Or for night to fall. [*Pause.*] We have kept our appointment, and that's an end to that. We are not saints, but we have kept our appointment. How many people can boast as much?

ESTRAGON: Billions.

VLADIMIR: You think so?

ESTRAGON: I don't know.

VLADIMIR: You may be right.

POZZO: Help!

VLADIMIR: All I know is that the hours are long, under these conditions, and constrain us to beguile them with proceedings which—how shall I say—which may at first sight seem reasonable, until they become a habit. You may say it is to prevent our reason from foundering. No doubt. But has it not long been straying in the night without end of the abyssal depths? That's what I sometimes wonder. You follow my reasoning?

ESTRAGON: [*aphoristic for once*]. We all are born mad. Some remain so.

(pp.79–80)

A few general comments on commentary technique may be helpful before embarking on this particular example.

Sometimes an examination question may explicitly require comment to be produced on particular points, such as themes, characterisation or structure. If it does, the answer should be limited to those points and no others, and evidence logically marshalled and presented under each one. It used to be common to ask for comment on 'form and content' or 'style and ideas' as two distinct categories. Since the work of Beckett and similar writers has entered the cultural stream, critics have generally become more aware that a concept cannot be separated from the language it comes in, and the two *must* be discussed simultaneously.

Where no guidance is given, there is a simple but effective pattern to follow, not only for the initial teasing-out of the threads of the text but also for the final writing-up of the answer.

1. Where the passage is from a known text, first set it briefly (*briefly*) in *context*.
2. State the *theme* of the passage: that is, its overall unifying idea or argument.
3. Isolate the *subject or subjects* through which the theme is given concrete form: that is, the imaginative peg on which the idea is hung.
4. '*Block out*' the passage, as a painter blocks out a painting, stating what are the major movements, or units of sense, through which it develops. This will enable useful comments to be made about general structure (whether there is a dramatic move to a climax, a simple static set of descriptions, or whatever). It will also enable Step 5 to be followed through without the discussion degenerating into incoherent fragments. It will surprise no-one who has read Beckett that commentary passages very often fall into two or, more often, three parts; the examiner's sense of order is as much

conditioned by doublets and triplets as anyone else's. If, however, the piece set is one of the desultory conversations, do not be afraid to call it so: 'loosely-structured', 'meandering', 'disconnected', 'fragmented', are all acceptable terms.

5. Go through each unit *line by line*, commenting on the implications of every relevant phrase. Point out recurring images or structural patterns as they occur. Refer back or forward in the drama to similar or connected incidents – but never lose the focus on the text that has been set. A commentary is not an essay.

6. Conclude the commentary by placing the text back into its *context* again, summing up its content and explaining how it is related to what happens next.

The passage set for discussion occurs in the middle section of Act 2. Pozzo and Lucky, the former now blind and the latter dumb, have reappeared on stage, only to trip over each other and fall in a heap. Vladimir and Estragon are now debating whether to respond to Pozzo's cries for help and pull them up.

Beckett's underlying theme is the emptiness (the vacuity) and the danger of 'discourse'. Language has no grip on reality. Instead of describing what is happening, it misrepresents it or pushes it to one side. It prevents action, instead of producing it. Vladimir claims his subject is the need for swift action. In fact, he himself wastes time in idle words, and nothing is done. Intentions and utterances slide in contradictory directions, 'in this immense confusion'.

The text falls roughly into three sections. Vladimir's first speech, to which Estragon makes no answer, is a pastiche (an imitation) of classical rhetoric, declaiming the dignity of mankind. Like Lucky's speech, it is a collection of clichés. He interrupts himself in full flight with the unexpected recollection of the appointment with Godot which is never far from his thoughts; Estragon joins in at this point, and the language drops down to earth. The third section is again mostly Vladimir's rhetoric, this time turned to a pessimistic discourse on the decay of reason.

Estragon's stillness and silence in the first section are a dramatic contrast to Vladimir's 'vehement' oratorical delivery. The mind may rant on, but the body takes no action. As Vladimir had said previously, of thought, 'we could have done without it'. Having 'the chance' to do something is a rare and precious occurrence, which one should be alert to seize. Vladimir and Estragon, bound up in their patterns of habit, never recognise chances, and let them slip by. In this, they are far more representative of mankind than they are aware ('But at this place, at this moment in time, all mankind is us, whether we like it or not'). Vladimir's words assume that they are standing in for mankind as hero. In fact, they represent man conscripted to his destiny ('whether we like it or not') and eternally missing his chance of greatness.

Vladimir's rhetoric, which should inspire confidence, in fact creates unease. It rings just slightly cracked. There are slightly too many inversions and too many repetitions building to a would-be imposing climax. Phrases like 'Foul brood', 'cruel fate', are too theatrical to be convincing. The rhetoric is undermined also by colloquialisms: 'Whether we like it not'; 'weigh the pros and cons'. Like Pozzo in his version of the twilight, Vladimir cannot control his styles.

The rolling echoes of rhetoric try to disguise the fact that what is being said makes no sense. There is no way in which one can 'represent worthily' a 'foul brood'. It is not clear what the example of the tiger is supposed to illustrate, nor whether the animal who thinks or the animal who doesn't think is supposed to be the model to follow. It would seem that acting after 'weigh[ing] the pros and cons' or acting 'without the least reflection' produce much the same result: anything could happen. Echoes of the indecisive, ineffective Hamlet, the great romantic hero of European culture, enter the discourse as Vladimir wrestles with the dignity of thought, deciding what is 'the question'. If your cultural hero is Hamlet, the text hints, you are doomed to failure.

Hamlet's answer to 'the question' (for him, 'To be or not to be') was his own death. For Vladimir, the answer is Godot, who, he suddenly realises, is the proper subject of his 'idle discourse'.

The whole situation now focuses on 'Godot'. Even Estragon's attention is caught ('Ah!'), and even Pozzo, in his new vulnerability, will grasp at this straw ('Help!'). But Vladimir hesitates, caught by his usual uncertainty. It is not sure that salvation will come with Godot. Night might fall instead (as it always does). Yet having spoken the unpalatable truth, Vladimir, as always, promptly represses it. He says that it doesn't matter that what they do inevitably ends in failure and disappointment. What matters is that they have 'kept their appointment', done what they thought they were supposed to. This, Vladimir claims, makes them unique; how many others, he asks, can 'boast' as much? Estragon's deflating 'Billions' makes plain the proper, and unflattering, sense in which the couple are 'representative of mankind'. As he said earlier, mankind consists of gullible, obedient fools: 'People are bloody ignorant apes'.

This central section concludes with a sudden finality, as each character sounds the single note that represents his 'essential' character. Estragon is a total blank ('I don't know'); Vladimir hesitates ('You may be right'); Pozzo demands support ('Help!'). Beckett's entire play is summed up at this point. The idea of Godot is at the centre of a great deal of apparent activity, which is, however, nothing but empty words. No character in a landscape dominated by Godot ever does anything but repeat its old, fixed role.

Vladimir, as always, is irrepressible. In the third section, he bursts into speech again, replacing the silence of despair with words about despair. This is not, perhaps, much of an advance, but is at least something slightly different, which is as much as he and Estragon ever manage.

There are some strange resonances in this third movement. The opening phrase ('All I know is . . . '), which seems at first to be a simple clearing of the throat, suddenly strikes us as a phrase to be taken literally and seriously. All Vladimir *does* know is that time seems long and they spend it looking for diversions. Similarly, 'how shall I say', 'You may say', begin to stand out sharply, with a particular significance. 'Saying' – playing with idle discourse – is the couple's sole occupation.

In his remarks on human reason, Vladimir again states the true nature of their situation and promptly suppresses it. In the effort to seem sane, they behave like lunatics. The distractions through which they try to forget their misery (waiting for Godot is just one of them) are never successful; but they become habits, and these habits are crazy. Vladimir uses all kinds of elaborate phrases to avoid using the word 'mad' ('to prevent our reason from foundering'; '[reason] long straying in the night without end of the abyssal depths'). Not only will he not say the word, he even continues to insist he is a man of reason, asking Estragon: 'You follow my reasoning?' Estragon speaks the word bluntly, but even he dodges the issue ('We are all born mad, etc.) If 'Some' remain mad, then others do not, and there is always the possibility he and Vladimir may be among them.

What happens after this passage is that the silence imposed by Estragon's statement is broken at once by the only kind of words that really matter. Pozzo calls, 'Help! I'll pay you!'. Estragon has the right answer: 'How much?' There is a clear contrast between the confused, empty words with which Vladimir and Estragon fill the silence of their lives and the true substance of the mad world they live in, which is the crude reality of money.

6 THE CRITICS' RECEPTION OF BECKETT'S PLAY

The following extracts indicate the range of questions raised by Beckett's drama and the diverse, even contradictory, positions critics have taken on them.

HAS 'GODOT' A CHRISTIAN DIMENSION?

A modern morality play, on permanent Christian themes. (G. S. Fraser, *Times Literary Supplement*, 10 February 1956)

The plays of Samuel Beckett abound in religious (particularly Christian) imagery and thought. As Beckett himself has remarked: 'Christianity is a mythology with which I am perfectly familiar, so I naturally use it'. But to conclude, therefore, that Beckett is a Christian dramatist – if one means by that statement that he espouses an essentially Christian point of view, and not simply that he deals with certain obviously Christian motifs – is surely to misjudge on the most fundamental level the significance of the plays' religious reference. Far from offering hope of religious consolation, Beckett's drama is a *kyrie eleison* of suffering and despair. (Hersh Zeifman, 'Religious Imagery in the Plays of Samuel Beckett' in R. Cohn ed., *Samuel Beckett: A Collection of Criticism*, 1975, pp. 93–94)

Existence depends on those metaphysical Micawbers who will go on waiting, against all rational argument, for something which may one day turn up to explain the purpose of living. Twenty years ago Mr Odets had us waiting for Lefty, the social messiah; less naively, Mr Beckett bids us wait for Godot, the spiritual signpost. (Kenneth Tynan, *The Observer*, 7 August 1955)

IS 'GODOT' THEATRE?

A play that can be recommended, provided we make clear that there is almost nothing in it that resembles what we usually call theatre. (Gabriel Marcel, *Les Nouvelles Littéraires*, 15 January 1953)

We find ourselves surprised and impressed that on such an abstract and general subject as the tedium of life, the vain quest for God and the stubborn search for happiness a writer could have written such a cruel, funny, living play. (Renée Saurel, *Les Lettres françaises*, 15 January 1953)

HAS 'GODOT' A MESSAGE?

It was a expression . . . by an author who expects each member of his audience to draw his own conclusion, make his own errors. It forced no dramatized moral on the viewer, it held out no specific hope. (C. Brandman, *San Quentin News*, cit. Alec Reid in R. Cohn (ed.), *Samuel Beckett*: *A Collection of Criticism*, 1975, p.65)

'GODOT': A PESSIMISTIC OR AN OPTIMISTIC PLAY?

Godot or the Music-Hall Sketch of Pascal's *Pensées* as played by the Fratellini Clowns. (Jean Anouilh, *Arts*, 27 February 1953) [Beckett's] pursuit of an immediate, necessary artistic truth, cut off from all social preoccupations, reveals a frank pessimism . . . [T]his is theatre turning back to itself and its origins in the mediaeval Christian world: an *Everyman* where man's final desolation and nakedness find neither consolation nor compensation. (J.-J. Mayoux, *Etudes anglaises*, October 1957)

What Vladimir and Estragon remind one of most forcibly is not tramps, but clowns: Footit and Chocolat, Alex and Zavatta, Pipo and Rhum of the Fratellini trio, the Marx Brothers, or the traditional comics of the English music-hall . . . It's all a game in *Godot*, but because the game is the only margin that still separates the protagonists from the nothingness, the only weapon left to fight the void, to endure the unbearable waiting, their playing takes on an intense vitality – like the movements of a man facing drowning, struggling between waves to hold his breath and save his skin. (Geneviève Serreau, *Histoire du nouveau Théâtre*, 1966)

'GODOT' AND THE MODERN WORLD

It would be ridiculous to think that people engaged in the real process of constructing their own destinies and confident in the future should want to go to the theatre . . . to meet up with Samuel Beckett's characters, night after night, by a lonely tree, in a wasteland, to wait in absurd self-abnegation for the arrival of a so-called Godot who nobody knows. What have such people to do with this Godot? and how can we possibly imagine *them*, the owners of one-sixth of the world, cast out and fastened away in this deadly, desolate wasteland, forgotten by men and gods? (Evgeni Sourkov, cit. P. Mélèse, *Samuel Beckett*, 1966)

Not many of us will have waited, evening after evening, by a tree on a country road for man who does not come, but again and again in our daily life we find ourselves in situations where we cannot act because we cannot get the knowledge essential to a decision. We have all chafed at the end of a telephone when it seemed the switchboard operator had forgotten us, or raged at an airport over unexplained delays to our plane. 'I think', said Beckett in 1956, 'anyone nowadays who pays the slightest attention to his own experience of a non-knower, a non-can-er' (i.e., of someone ignorant, therefore impotent). The world-wide appeal of *Godot* would seem to bear him out. (A. Reid, op. cit.)

The real destructive nihilism acted out in the [extermination] camps was expressed artistically only in works like Beckett's *Endgame* or *Waiting for Godot*, in which the naked unaccommodated man is reduced to the role of helpless, hopeless, impotent comic, who talks and talks and talks in order to postpone for a while the silence of his own desolation. (A. Alvarez, cit. Eric Bentley, 1967, – in *The Critical Heritage*)

[To] see Beckett as a victim of bourgeois society and capitalism goes right against all this writer's work and thought. Samuel Beckett does not suffer from the social and political condition but from our existential condition, man's metaphysical situation. Such unease is inherent in the human condition. All societies are bad, all humanity and all creation have lived in sorrow from the very

beginning of the world . . . Man's tragic situation, the unhappi-
ness of life, is a fact that comes from neither capitalism nor
Judeo-Christian thought. (E. Ionesco, 'A propos de Beckett', cit.
Cahiers de l'Herne, 1976, p.149)

A NEW VIEW OF TIME

Plato remarks in his *Timaeus* that:

Past and future are categories of time that we ourselves have
created and that we attribute, wrongly and unthinkingly, to the
eternal essence. We say 'was', 'is', 'will be' but the truth is that
only 'is' can be used in any adequate fashion.

And *Godot* is an exciting attempt to smash these 'categories'
which have left such a mark on everyday language and to
re-establish in us some sense of the 'eternal essence' they normally
stop us from seeing . . . [But Beckett] doesn't speak of the
essence, he only speaks about its threshold, that area of being
where existence and essence, I and not-I, the temporal and the out
of time, co-exist for eternity, in the strange, ambiguous, fatal
world of half-exile which for Beckett is the image of our condition.
(Ross Chambers, 'Beckett, man of extreme situations', *Cahiers
Renaud-Barrault*, No.44, October 1963)

LANGUAGE IN 'GODOT': ALL OR NOTHING?

In *Waiting for Godot*, Beckett . . . had, so to speak, won a bet
with himself: to make us accept in the theatre the spectacle of pure
speech, in defiance of the law of the theatre that says a spectacle is
always an event. The wait for the invisible Godot, on which people
wasted considerable time looking for a symbolic interpretation,
had one purpose only: to open up a completely empty stretch of
time. It was within the frame of that empty stretch that the real
subject of the play emerged: the unfolding of speech. He pulled it
off brilliantly. A stage where nothing happened, transformed into
the fascinating place where the loneliness of language was rev-
ealed. (Jean Vannier, 'Fin de partie', in *Théâtre populaire*, No.25,
July 1957)

What does *Waiting for Godot* have to offer? Saying nothing happens is not saying much. In any case, other playwrights have already staged plays without action and plot. What you have to say here is 'Less than nothing', as though we were watching a kind of regression beyond nothing . . . 'This is becoming really insignificant', one of the friends says in this context. 'Not enough', says the other. And his reply is punctuated by a long silence.

From start to finish the dialogue is *dying*, worn out, permanently situated on those frontiers of death where all Beckett's 'heroes' exist . . . In the general collapse, there is a kind of high-point – or actually the opposite of a high-point: a low point, absolute rock-bottom. . . . No a single character is left standing. All there is on the stage is the squirming, whining heap, and then you see Didi's face light up and he declares, in a voice almost calm again: 'We are men!'

We were familiar with the theatre of ideas . . . It was a bit dull, but there was some solid 'thought', in the audience and on-stage. Thought, even subversive thought, is always reassuring. Language – fine language – is reassuring too. Just think how many misunderstandings noble, harmonious discourse has created, a mask for ideas and a mask for their absence.

Here there is no misunderstanding, and no more thought than fine language. Both of them figure in the text only in the form of parody . . . or corpse. (Alain Robbe-Grillet, *Pour un nouveau roman*, Paris, 1963)

7 BECKETT'S RECEPTION
OF THE CRITICS

I feel the only line is to refuse to be involved in exegesis of any kind. And to insist on the extreme simplicity of dramatic situation and issue . . . we have no elucidation to offer of mysteries that are all of [journalists'] making. My work is a matter of fundamental sounds (no joke intended) made as fully as possible and I accept responsibility for nothing else. If people want to have headaches among the overtones, let them. And provide their own aspirin. (Beckett, letter to Alan Schneider, 12 August 1957, cit. Reid, p.66)

[I]n winter, under my greatcoat, I wrapped myself in swathes of newspaper, and did not shed them until the earth awoke, for good, in April. The *Times Literary Supplement* was admirably adapted to this purpose, of a never failing toughness and impenetrability. Even farts made no impression on it. (*Molloy*, p.29)

REVISION QUESTIONS

1. Asked 'Who or what does Godot mean?' Beckett answered, 'If I knew, I would have said so in the play.' What clues have you found in your reading of the text?

2. Compare and contrast the relationship between Vladimir and Estragon with that between Pozzo and Lucky.

3. What is new about Beckett's concept of (a) plot; (b) character? Does it make good theatre?

4. 'The dialogue is studded with words that have no meaning for normal ears' (Harold Hobson). Do you agree?

5. Discuss the importance of the unexpected in Beckett's theatre.

6. 'You can't enjoy Waiting for Godot unless someone explains it first'. Do you agree?

7. Describe and discuss the humour of Waiting for Godot.

8. 'A theatre of silence'. Discuss this description of Beckett's drama, with special reference to Waiting for Godot.

9. Discuss the presentation of (a) time; (b) memory; (c) reason in Waiting for Godot.

10. 'A pantomine'; 'a circus'; 'a scream'. How well do these terms apply to Waiting for Godot, and which, if any, do you think the most appropriate?

FURTHER READING

This bibliography contains only those works which have been quoted
from in the text or drawn on frequently. It does not include critics
quoted in Chapter 6, where full references are given. The most useful
texts are asterisked.

*Bair, D., *Samuel Beckett: A Biography* (Jonathan Cape, 1978).

Beer, A., '*Watt*, Knott and Beckett's Bilingualism', *Journal of
Beckett Studies* (John Calder (Publishers) Ltd and the Beckett
Archive at the University of Reading), No.10, 1985.

Cahiers de l'Herne, (ed.) Tom Bishop and Raymond Felderman
(Editions de l'Herne, 1976).

Cohn, R. (ed.), *Samuel Beckett: A Collection of Criticism*
(McGraw-Hill, 1975).

— , 'Beckett's German *Godot*', *Journal of Beckett Studies*, No. 1,
Winter 1976.

* — , *Just Play: Beckett's Theatre* (Princeton University Press,
1980).

*Esslin, M., *The Theatre of the Absurd*, rev. ed. (Penguin, 1983).

Fletcher, J. and Spurling, J., *Beckett: A Study of his Plays,* 2nd ed.
(Eyre Methuen, 1972).

Graver, L., and Federman, R. (eds), *Samuel Beckett: The Critical
Heritage* (Routledge & Kegan Paul, 1979).

Mélèse, P, *Samuel Beckett* (Editions Seghers, 1966).

Mercier, V., *Beckett/Beckett: The Truth of Contradictions* (Oxford
University Press, 1977).

Reid, A., 'From Beginning to Date: Some Thoughts on the Plays of
Samuel Beckett', in R. Cohn (ed.), *op. cit*

Robbe-Grillet, A., *Pour un nouveau roman* (Editions de Minuit,
1963).

Schneider, A., 'On directing *Film*', essay pub. after S. Beckett, *Film*
(Grove Press Inc., 1969).

Simpson, A, *Beckett and Behan and a Theatre in Dublin* (Routledge
& Kegan Paul, 1962).

Zeifman, H., 'Religious Imagery in the Plays of Samuel Beckett', in R. Cohn (ed.), *op.cit.*

Zilliacus, Claus, *Beckett and Broadcasting* (Abo Academi, 1976).

— , 'Beckett v. Brecht in Helsinki, 1979', *Journal of Beckett Studies*, No.6, Autumn 1980.

*   *   *   *   *

Mastering English Literature
Richard Gill

Mastering English Literature will help readers both to enjoy
English Literature and to be successful in 'O' levels, 'A' levels
and other public exams. It is an introduction to the study of
poetry, novels and drama which helps the reader in four ways –
by providing ways of approaching literature, by giving examples
and practice exercises, by offering hints on how to write about
literature, and by the author's own evident enthusiasm for the
subject. With extracts from more than 200 texts, this is an
enjoyable account of how to get the maximum satisfaction out
of reading, whether it be for formal examinations or simply
for pleasure.

Work Out English Literature ('A' level)
S.H. Burton

This book familiarises 'A' level English Literature candidates
with every kind of test which they are likely to encounter.
Suggested answers are worked out step by step and accompanied by full author's commentary. The book helps students
to clarify their aims and establish techniques and standards so
that they can make appropriate responses to similar questions
when the examination pressures are on. It opens up fresh ways
of looking at the full range of set texts, authors and critical
judgements and motivates students to know more of these
matters.

THE MACMILLAN SHAKESPEARE

General Editor: PETER HOLLINDALE
Advisory Editor: PHILIP BROCKBANK

The Macmillan Shakespeare features:
* clear and uncluttered texts with modernised punctuation and spelling wherever possible;
* full explanatory notes printed on the page facing the relevant text for ease of reference;
* stimulating introductions which concentrate on content, dramatic effect, character and imagery, rather than mere dates and sources.

Above all, The Macmillan Shakespeare treats each play as a work for the theatre which can also be enjoyed on the page.

CORIOLANUS
Editor: Tony Parr

THE WINTER'S TALE
Editor: Christopher Parry

MUCH ADO ABOUT NOTHING
Editor: Jan McKeith

RICHARD II
Editor: Richard Adams

RICHARD III
Editor: Richard Adams

HENRY IV, PART I
Editor: Peter Hollindale

HENRY IV, PART II
Editor: Tony Parr

HENRY V
Editor: Brian Phythian

AS YOU LIKE IT
Editor: Peter Hollindale

A MIDSUMMER NIGHT'S DREAM
Editor: Norman Sanders

THE MERCHANT OF VENICE
Editor: Christopher Parry

THE TAMING OF THE SHREW
Editor: Robin Hood

TWELFTH NIGHT
Editor: E. A. J. Honigmann

THE TEMPEST
Editor: A. C. Spearing

ROMEO AND JULIET
Editor: James Gibson

JULIUS CAESAR
Editor: D. R. Elloway

MACBETH
Editor: D. R. Elloway

HAMLET
Editor: Nigel Alexander

ANTONY AND CLEOPATRA
Editors: Jan McKeith and
Richard Adams

OTHELLO
Editors: Celia Hilton and R. T. Jones

KING LEAR
Editor: Philip Edwards

MACMILLAN STUDENTS' NOVELS

General Editor: JAMES GIBSON

The Macmillan Students' Novels are low-priced, new editions of major classics, aimed at the first examination candidate. Each volume contains:

* enough explanation and background material to make the novels accessible — and rewarding — to pupils with little or no previous knowledge of the author or the literary period;

* detailed notes elucidate matters of vocabulary, interpretation and historical background;

* eight pages of plates comprising facsimiles of manuscripts and early editions, portraits of the author and photographs of the geographical setting of the novels.

JANE AUSTEN: MANSFIELD PARK
Editor: Richard Wirdnam

JANE AUSTEN: NORTHANGER ABBEY
Editor: Raymond Wilson

JANE AUSTEN: PRIDE AND PREJUDICE
Editor: Raymond Wilson

JANE AUSTEN: SENSE AND SENSIBILITY
Editor: Raymond Wilson

JANE AUSTEN: PERSUASION
Editor: Richard Wirdnam

CHARLOTTE BRONTË: JANE EYRE
Editor: F. B. Pinion

EMILY BRONTË: WUTHERING HEIGHTS
Editor: Graham Handley

JOSEPH CONRAD: LORD JIM
Editor: Peter Hollindale

CHARLES DICKENS: GREAT EXPECTATIONS
Editor: James Gibson

CHARLES DICKENS: HARD TIMES
Editor: James Gibson

CHARLES DICKENS: OLIVER TWIST
Editor: Guy Williams

CHARLES DICKENS: A TALE OF TWO CITIES
Editor: James Gibson

GEORGE ELIOT: SILAS MARNER
Editor: Norman Howlings

GEORGE ELIOT: THE MILL ON THE FLOSS
Editor: Graham Handley

D. H. LAWRENCE: SONS AND LOVERS
Editor: James Gibson

D. H. LAWRENCE: THE RAINBOW
Editor: James Gibson

MARK TWAIN: HUCKLEBERRY FINN
Editor: Christopher Parry

MACMILLAN SHAKESPEARE VIDEO WORKSHOPS

DAVID WHITWORTH

Three unique book and video packages, each examining a particular aspect of Shakespeare's work; tragedy, comedy and the Roman plays. Designed for all students of Shakespeare, each package assumes no previous knowledge of the plays and can serve as a useful introduction to Shakespeare for 'O' and 'A' level candidates as well as for students at colleges and institutes of further, higher and adult education.

The material is based on the New Shakespeare Company Workshops at the Roundhouse, adapted and extended for television. By combining the resources of television and a small theatre company, this exploration of Shakespeare's plays offers insights into varied interpretations, presentation, styles of acting as well as useful background information.

While being no substitute for seeing the whole plays in performance, it is envisaged that these video cassettes will impart something of the original excitement of the theatrical experience, and serve as a welcome complement to textual analysis leading to an enriched and broader view of the plays.

Each package consists of:

* the Macmillan Shakespeare editions of the plays concerned;

* a video cassette available in VHS or Beta;

* a leaflet of teacher's notes.

THE TORTURED MIND
looks at the four tragedies Hamlet, Othello, Macbeth and King Lear.

THE COMIC SPIRIT
examines the comedies Much Ado About Nothing, Twelfth Night, A Midsummer Night's Dream, and As You Like It.

THE ROMAN PLAYS
Features Julius Caesar, Antony and Cleopatra
and Coriolanus